LETTS CREATIVE NEEDLECRAFTS

# COUNTED
# CROSS STITCH

·ANGELA·WAINWRIGHT·

LETTS CREATIVE NEEDLECRAFTS

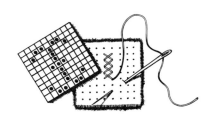

# COUNTED CROSS STITCH

## ANGELA WAINWRIGHT

CHARLES LETTS · Letts · FOUNDED 1796

First published 1990
by Charles Letts & Company Ltd
Diary House, Borough Road
London SE1 1DW

Designed and produced by Rosemary Wilkinson
30 Blackroot Road, Sutton Coldfield, B74 2QP

Reprinted in 1991

**Editor**: Lorna Rogerson
**Illustrators**: Anthony Jones and Elsa Godfrey
**Design coordinator**: Patrick Knowles
**Designer**: Mike Spiller
**Photographer**: Linear Photographic
**Cover photograph**: Pablo Keller

© Charles Letts & Company Ltd 1990

CIP catalogue record for this book is available from the British Library

ISBN 1 85238 105 1

Typeset by Fakenham Photosetting Ltd, Fakenham, Norfolk

Printed in Belgium

# CONTENTS

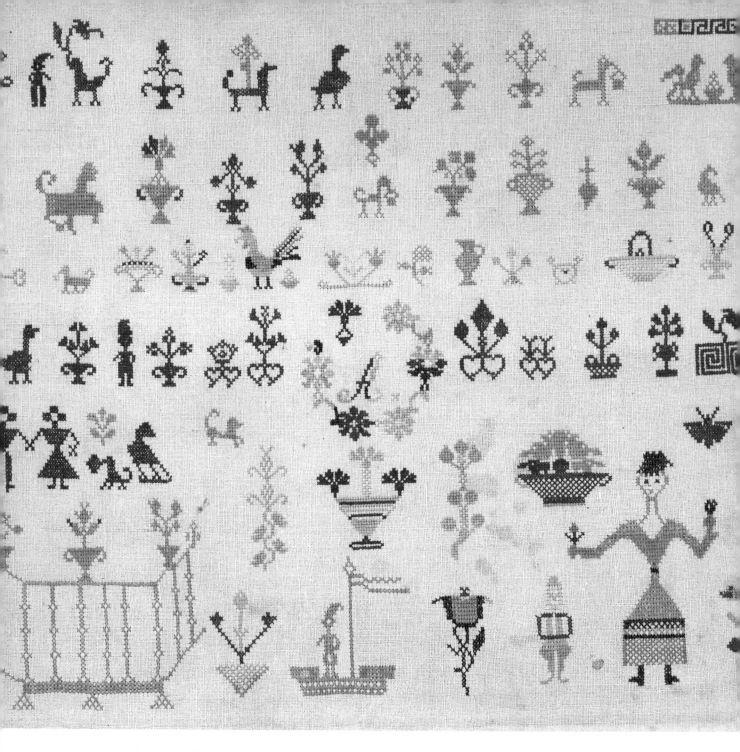

*A section of a spot sampler, thought to have been worked in Pennsylvania in the 19th century*

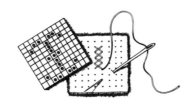

# DESIGN:
# PAST AND PRESENT

The history of the cross stitch from practical uses on clothing in
its early days to the sampler – for education, instruction and
pure display.

Cross stitch is a very ancient art. In early civilizations it was the first effective way of lacing pieces of animal skin together and throughout the Ancient World cross stitch was used as a functional and decorative art on clothing and on household goods. It was usually worked in large colourful motifs using wool on woollen or linen cloth.

The three most fundamental features of cross stitch – that it is practical; simple in construction and aesthetically pleasing – ensured its survival through the centuries and underlie its development within different cultures around the world. The precise means by which the skill spread from country to country is disputed but it is undeniably a part of the embroidery heritage in countries as far apart as Mexico and the Netherlands, Greece, India and Thailand. Each country has its own distinctive designs but all use the simple cross stitch to achieve them.

In Europe cross stitch became established as an embroidery stitch in the sixteenth century, when it was mostly worked by ladies of the court. The embroidery embellished household items and it was a sign of status. The use of a needle thus became one of the first skills taught to young girls in primary schools.

Skilled needlewomen would keep records of their favourite patterns and stitches and the girls would learn their techniques from these pieces. These pattern records were called by the now familiar term 'sampler', from the Old French 'exemplaire', which in turn derived from the Latin word 'exemplum', meaning copy or pattern. A sampler (the words 'saumpler' and 'exemplar' were also used) was therefore either a piece of canvas stitched by a beginner as a practice piece or a complex hanging embroidered by a competent needlewoman to celebrate her skills.

From this point the history of cross stitch is

very much the history of the sampler. The earliest dated sampler known of in Britain can be seen at the Victoria & Albert Museum in London. It is signed 'Jane Bostocke' and dated 1598. Most samplers of this period were not so helpfully recorded, and although there are many samplers to be found in museums and in private collections, it is impossible to date them accurately. However, the types of pattern, fabric and silks can provide certain valuable clues. Some samplers may well be older than Jane's efforts of 1598, but they can be dated only approximately.

These early pieces are known as 'random' or 'spot' samplers due to the fact that the patterns were worked in a non-symmetrical fashion with the motifs scattered over the fabric. They were almost always worked on linen fabric using silk, gold or silver threads. Obviously not the work of a needlewoman in a poor household! They were usually large pieces, perhaps two feet in length and one foot wide and were covered in a wide variety of motifs and stitches. Up to ten different stitches, including the mainstay of this book, simple cross stitch, could be found on one sampler alone.

The skill of these embroiderers is also demonstrated in the enormous range of motifs stitched, ranging from domestic to fantastical, from wild flowers to household implements and including every plant that ever grew in an Elizabethan garden. Each sampler was also personalized with words or objects specific to one particular family; an art we can all copy in our own sampler work.

*A Danish sampler completed in 1798*

Though the majority of the pieces that have survived are most probably the work of the higher social scales, the work of the lower social orders was, I am sure, just as beautiful, though perhaps not as complex. It was of necessity more practical in its application, for use on household and personal items, which were inevitably subject to harder wear with the result that few examples have survived. This practical use of the cross stitch led to it often being called 'marker' stitch.

We are still fortunate in being able to admire cross stitch domestic work in the form of small motifs which have been sewn, then appliquéd onto such items as bed hangings, examples can be viewed in some of the stately homes of England.

Gradually the 'spot' patterns died out and by the seventeenth century alphabets and numbers began to be included. The work was often signed and dated and most pieces seem to be the work of children. Figures and flower motifs predominate.

By the eighteenth century and remaining in style for about 150 years, what we now think of as the conventional sampler was the fashion. It was shorter in length, wider and there was a greater experimentation with fabric types: cotton, silk gauze and tammy cloth (a fine woollen fabric) were all used. Stitches were not quite as varied or as complex as before and the simple cross stitch was more often favoured. Overall design became perhaps more important than the skill of stitchery. Eventually, simple cross stitch was being used almost to the exclusion of other stitches. Border patterns became dominant and so too did alphabets. In addition to their function as needlework practice, these pieces were also used as learning aids for other subjects. Alphabets and numbers were rehearsed through this medium.

Alphabets gave way during the nineteenth century to pious thoughts and religious texts – how often have I looked at these lovely old pictures and wondered at their influence on the late nineteenth century child.

However, all was not doom and gloom. Some samplers are to be found, particularly in the United States, depicting maps – cross stitch was becoming the fun way to learn geography.

The increase in trade and inter-marriage between the people of Europe and the movement of people in the ever-expanding world, are clearly reflected in cross stitch work. French, Spanish, Dutch and Danish influences were, and continue to be, apparent in British pieces.

As already mentioned, American samplers developed along distinctive lines, having been introduced by settlers from Britain and often taught in private schools by British needlewomen. Similarly in Australia, samplers were first made by the new settlers but gradually Australian motifs and emblems were incorporated into the pictures.

As the sampler developed it became lighter in tone, the choice of subject for its motifs became wider and the form more varied: favoured pets, much-loved family and homes might well be included. All were uniquely personalized thus providing a lasting family record and incidentally a valuable piece of social history – lucky the family which still has one of these heirlooms in its possession.

After a decline in popularity coinciding with the development of machine-made textiles, the sampler is now regaining a proper place in the embroidery world. The antique pieces are admired and collected as a social record and new pieces are worked as personal commemorative pieces. In our busy lives the therapeutic effect of working cross stitch is greatly valued and the results of the labours much appreciated. So, happy stitching! Remember your pieces of work will be tomorrow's heirlooms.

## BASIC EQUIPMENT

Choosing the right equipment is very important. The three essentials for any embroidery: fabric, thread and needle, are listed below with advice on what is most suitable for cross stitch work. Apart from these, a pair of good embroidery or small, sharp-pointed scissors is essential. Frames are less vital but their uses are explained below.

## FABRICS

**Even-weave**  The most popular type of fabric for cross stitch. Even-weave is so-called because in any measured square inch (or centimetre) of fabric, the number of warp and weft threads is exactly the same. It comes in a variety of sizes and types. The sizes are graded according to the number of threads per inch (or centimetre) with the highest number denoting the finest weave and therefore producing the smallest stitches. It is possible to buy fabric with 10 threads to the inch or 36 threads to the inch and all grades in between.

'Binca' or 'Bincarette' is the name given to even-weave fabric with 10 threads to the inch. It produces large, bold, open designs most suitable for educational purposes but not recommended for a prospective needlewoman attempting an heirloom. However, if children wish to try some of the simpler designs in this book, 'Binca' is a good fabric to start with. The finished project will then be greatly

increased in size and a different thickness of thread will be necessary, as detailed below.

'Aida' is an even-weave fabric in which the weft and warp threads have been bulked together and woven as one unit, creating clearly defined holes through which to pass the needle. All the projects in this book have been worked on 'Aida' fabric with 14, 15, 18 or 22 threads to the inch or on 'Sal-EM', apart from the Breakfast Traycloth on page 86, for which a finer count of fabric has been used.

'Sal-EM' is a fabric produced in America, which is used for fine stitching but also is easily laundered and is therefore suitable for projects, such as handtowels, which require frequent washing. The 'Sal-EM' fabric used in this book has 26 threads to the inch.

'Hardanger' is another specialist type of even-weave fabric, in which pairs of threads are woven together.

*N.B. The number of threads to the inch is referred to as the 'count' of the fabric.*

**Linen**  This is a plain-weave fabric, i.e. the weft threads weave alternately over and under the warp threads. It is not an even-weave but can be used for fine cross stitching.

These fabrics come in a variety of colours, although the designs featured here are limited to either white or cream. These colours provide a most effective background to the stitch colours, as well as proving economical, since

fabric left over from one project will be suitable for the next. The even-weave fabrics are widely available at specialist shops (see also page 93). Most shops will be more than willing to cut small pieces and often keep a box of remnants perfect for small project work.

## THREADS

The whole spectrum of colours and a wide variety of types of thread can be found in most good needlecraft shops and departments or handicraft stores. The threads also vary in thickness. For this book I have used stranded cottons exclusively, as they adapt well to the different counts of fabric and are most widely available. Below are details on the number of strands to use with the various fabric counts, together with other types of threads suitable for cross stitch, in case you wish to experiment.

Take care to choose your shades in a good light. Many of the shades are very close in colour and artificial light alters them, particularly pinks and blues.

**Stranded cotton**  This is made up of six strands loosely twisted together. The strands can be separated and used in different combinations. On 10 to 16 count fabric use 3 strands; on 16 to 24 use 2 and on 24 to 36 use 1 strand.

**Crochet cotton**  A firmly-twisted thread in 2- or 4-ply. Use the 4-ply on counts of 10 to 20.

**Danish flower threads:** a specialist thread: on counts of 14 to 20 use two threads, on 20+ use one thread.

**Perlé cotton:** a glossy, twisted 2-ply thread. Use only on low counts.

**Coton à broder**   A highly-twisted, fine thread. Use on counts of 10 to 24.

**Silk threads**   Not always dye-fast, so take care to keep your work very clean. Suitable for very fine work, i.e. high count fabrics.

## NEEDLES

The best needle for cross stitch is a tapestry needle, its blunt end allows it to pass easily between the threads of the fabric without splitting them. Tapestry needles are available in a range of sizes from 13 to 26, with the highest number being the finest.

I like to use a size 24, or 22 on coarser-woven fabrics. A general rule is that the needle and thread should pass through the fabric without causing any distortion. The size of the eye of the needle should also be related to the thread. It should be large enough for the thread to pass through smoothly. If it is too small the thread will fray.

## FRAMES

Old samplers of very soft fabric were generally worked on a frame, which prevented the fabric from becoming distorted as it was stitched. Small pictures or designs worked on Aida, Binca or linen do not necessarily require a frame and I do not use a frame even for fairly large projects, unless the fabric is of a very high count or is very soft, as I prefer the greater manoeuvrability of the fabric possible without a frame. However, it is a matter of personal preference. If you feel more comfortable using a frame, I suggest a hoop or ring frame which will hold the fabric firmly between two rings, one clipping over the other. They come in a variety of sizes to suit the area being worked.

For very large projects a rotating frame, such as is used for needlepoint, can be useful.

**Beware, cross stitching is addictive! Below are some do's and don't's which apply to the general working of the projects. This is followed by instructions on specific techniques.**

Work only in a good light, particularly when stitching on a higher count fabric. An overhead lamp, if artificial light is necessary, is a great help. Fit the lamp with a daylight simulation bulb and you will find that it reduces eye strain and allows correct colour matching of threads.

Do not worry if Aida fabric becomes limp while you work it. Gentle pressing with a steam iron on the reverse over a padded surface after completion will revitalize and stiffen the fabric.

Before beginning to stitch a particular chart, fix a snippet of each shade of thread being used to a piece of paper with masking tape and write the number beside it. You could also write down the symbol used in the relevant chart as a record. This is invaluable if you are going to work in different lights.

Remember that colours will appear lighter on the work than in the skein.

If the chart is complex and you find you have difficulty in finding the exact place where you left off, gently pencil around the stitches you have completed. Do this lightly, so that you can still see the relationship of one stitch to another. The pencil marks can be erased once the project is completed, so that the chart can be used again.

If you are not using a frame and you find that your work is pulling slightly in one direction, ease your tension slightly. Once the work is finished you can wash the work in warm water and stretch it gently back into shape while damp.

For a first cross stitch piece, choose a project that is not too complex, i.e. one with a small design, with only a few different colours, and work with a good quality fabric.

Projects for all levels of ability are included in this book.

### TECHNIQUES

**Preparing the fabric**
When working larger pieces of fabric and particularly if you are not using a frame, the edges must be prevented from fraying. Do this

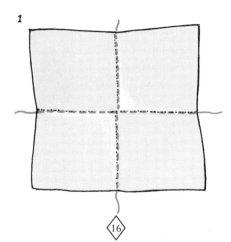

1

either by oversewing or by covering the edges with masking tape.

Next find the centre vertical thread by folding the fabric in half lengthwise. Mark this line with a row of tacking stitches. Fold the fabric in half crosswise to find the centre horizontal line and tack as before (diagram 1).

*N.B. With some of the small projects it may only be necessary to fold the fabric and crease it.*

The coloured lines on each of the charts accompanying the projects show the positioning of the centre vertical and horizontal lines. The exact point at which you start stitching is given with each individual project but in general for the larger projects you will be directed to start at the top centre stitch and for smaller projects it will be the centre stitch of the whole design.

**Beginning to stitch**
Thread the needle with no more than 35 cm (14 in) of cotton: longer lengths may fray or shred.

Do not knot the thread. Knots make the work lumpy and can unravel. To commence the first stitch, pull the thread through from the reverse of the fabric, leaving a 'tail' of thread of about 5 cm (2 in). Hold this 'tail' under the fabric while working the first stitch. After a few more stitches have been worked, the 'tail' can be darned into the stitches at the back of the work.

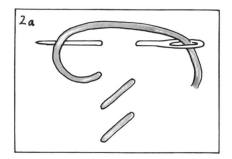

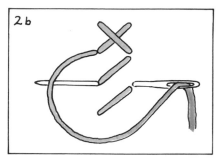

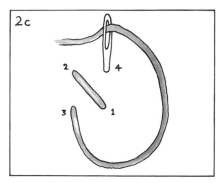

possible work in vertical rows beginning at the bottom. First work a row of half stitches as shown in diagram 2a, then working in the reverse direction, complete the cross (diagram 2b). If working a single cross stitch, follow the sequence in diagram 2c.

It is important that the top half of the stitches should all slant in the same direction, otherwise the work will be uneven.

*N.B. Unless otherwise stated, each stitch is worked over one count of the fabric throughout the projects.*

One square on the charts represents one stitch. Diagram 3 shows the relationship between the squares on the chart and the count of the fabric. If the colour layout of a particular design means that stitches in one colour are scattered in small

numbers across the work, rather than fastening off after each little block, take the thread through to the reverse of the work and remove the needle. Direct this thread away from the motif being worked and leave until you wish to use that shade again.

*N.B. This technique can only be used when these scattered stitches are separated by just three or four spaces, otherwise you will create bad tension in your work and unsightly lines all over the reverse. These lines may well show through a fabric with a low thread count.*

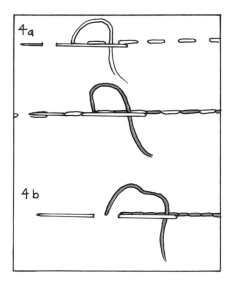

## Stitches

The simple cross stitch, which formed the basis of the later samplers, is the main stitch used in this book. Occasionally, where definition or a very fine line is needed, running stitch or back stitch is also used.

Cross stitch: to work a block of stitches in one colour, wherever

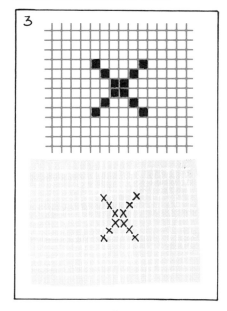

Running stitch: another basic stitch used for line work, whether for lettering or for detail. It is simple to work, as shown in diagram 4a.

Back stitch: an alternative to running stitch for line work. Follow diagram 4b to stitch.

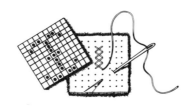

# BOOKMARKS

A group of five bookmarks designed for particular people and special books. An alphabet chart is given, so that the two named bookmarks and the floral design can be personalized, making ideal gifts. This is an easy project, quickly completed.

For the floral and the prayer bookmark: 2 lace-trimmed bookmarks (page 93)

For the named bookmarks: 3 piece of 15 count Aida band, 38 cm (15 in) long

*or* (if making your own bookmarks) 5 pieces of white or cream 18 count Aida fabric: each 4.5 × 18 cm (1¾ × 7 in) *and* for each piece of Aida fabric, 50 cm (½ yard) edging lace, 2 cm (¾ in) wide *plus* a little narrow ribbon to make a bow

Sewing thread to match fabric

Tapestry needle size 22 or 24

Stranded cotton as follows (note that some colours are used in more than one bookmark – one skein is sufficient for all):

**Floral bookmark**

| Colour | DMC | Anchor |
|---|---|---|
| Peach | 352 | 09 |
| Rose pink | 961 | 040 |
| Pale yellow | 445 | 0288 |
| Green | 954 | 0204 |
| Blue | 793 | 0121 |

**Prayer bookmark**

| | | |
|---|---|---|
| Brown | 433 | 0358 |
| Yellow | 307 | 0290 |
| Pink | 605 | 074 |
| Pale green | 954 | 0204 |

**Named bookmark – blue name**

| | | |
|---|---|---|
| Dark blue | 796 | 0133 |
| Red | 666 | 046 |
| Black | 310 | 0403 |
| Grey | 413 | 0400 |
| Yellow | 307 | 0290 |
| Green | 702 | 0227 |

**Named bookmark – red name**

| | | |
|---|---|---|
| Red | 666 | 046 |
| Yellow | 307 | 0290 |
| Green | 702 | 0227 |
| Dark blue | 796 | 0133 |
| Black | 310 | 0403 |
| Brown | 433 | 0358 |
| Pink | 605 | 074 |

**Bon Appetit**

| | | |
|---|---|---|
| Blue | 793 | 0121 |
| Brown | 433 | 0358 |
| Medium green | 562 | 209 |
| Dark red | 816 | 043 |
| Light grey | 3024 | 0391 |
| Dark grey | 317 | 0400 |
| Pink | 605 | 074 |
| Orange | 970 | 0925 |
| Dark green | 895 | 0269 |
| Sand | 436 | 0363 |

## Lace-edged bookmarks

Work the designs using two strands of cotton. Check the number of counts on the fabric you are using against the charts on page 23, which show 30 across and 120 down. Some ready-made bookmarks vary slightly in their count numbers. If there is a discrepancy, adjust the design accordingly from the centre of the chart.

Begin stitching at the point marked on the chart. Work the lettering (prayer bookmark) and the initials border (floral) in back or running stitch.

On the design for the floral bookmark, the central area has been left blank, so that an initial of your choice can be worked. Use the alphabet chart on page 21 and place the letter centrally.

To finish a pre-edged lacy bookmark, simply tidy the back of the work and press as necessary (page 92).

## Aida band bookmarks

For these bookmarks, the fabric is doubled over after the stitching is completed to provide a backing to the work.

Fold the fabric in half crosswise to find the centre and mark this with a line of tacking. Open out the fabric and work the design on the lower half only, following one of the charts on page 22.

Work the designs using two strands of cotton.

Once the design has been worked, fold the fabric again, right sides together and back stitch across the bottom short edge. Turn right side out and work one or two back stitches close to the edge at intervals along the length of the bookmark to enclose the design and join the two pieces together (diagram 1).

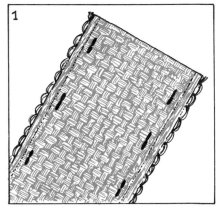

Still using two strands of cotton, cut 15 cm (6 in) lengths from all the colours used. Thread one of these lengths through the first hole at the left hand side of the bottom of the bookmark, so that it passes through the hole at the centre point of its length. Repeat this process with the other length in every other hole across the bottom of the piece and alternating the colours.

When you have worked across the band, tie all the lengths together attractively and trim the uneven ends (diagram 2).

## Making your own bookmarks

If Aida band or the ready-made lacy bookmarks are not available, it is

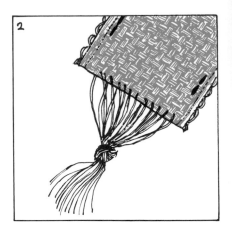

possible to make your own. This is a good way of using up left-over pieces of fabric and solves the problem of how to work a lengthy name that will not fit onto a pre-made bookmark.

Using one piece of Aida fabric 4.5 × 18 cm (1¾ × 7 in), lay on a flat surface, right side up. Starting in one corner, lay the lace over the edge of the bookmark, so that there is an overlap of 6 mm (¼ in) and

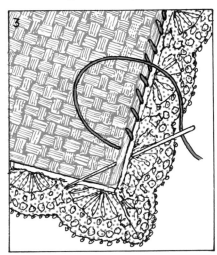

pin, folding the lace into a right angle at the corners.

To attach the lace, use a matching thread and oversew the edge of the lace with small, even-spaced stitches, using the holes of the Aida fabric as a guide to the placing of the stitches (diagram 3). Alternatively, the lace could be attached by machine, using a zig-zag stitch.

Neaten the ends of the lace, where they join up and trim the bottom of the bookmark with a bow made from the narrow ribbon, just catching it onto the Aida fabric.

Other motifs from projects featured in the following pages could be adapted for use on a bookmark. The hot air balloons and the yacht from the Modern Sampler (page 56), for example, or the napkin motif (page 91) could be repeated vertically with a border of single cross stitches in a matching colour. The cat and dog designs given on page 60 would make an appropriate bookmark for pet lovers.

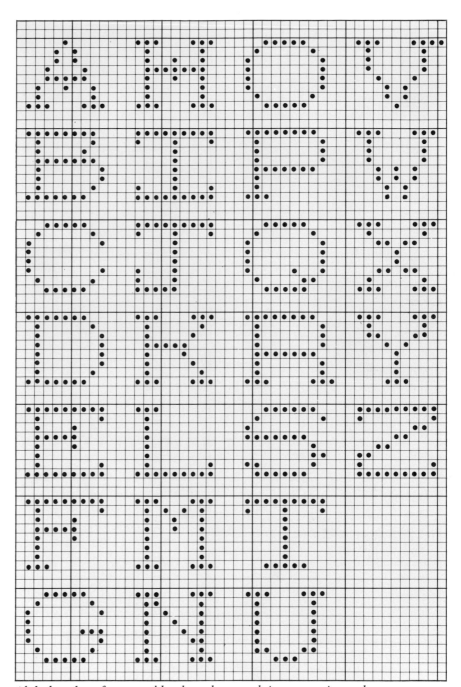

*Alphabet chart for named bookmarks – work in appropriate colour*

## KEYS

### Named bookmark – red

- ● Yellow
- × Green
- ○ Dark blue
- ■ Black
- ★ Pink
  Name in red
  Balloon strings in brown

### Named bookmark – blue

- − Red
- ■ Black
- ∧ Grey
- ● Yellow
- × Green
  Name in dark blue

### Floral bookmark

- ▲ Peach
- / Rose pink
- ● Pale yellow
- × Green
- ○ Blue
  Box in green

### Bon Appetit

- ○ Blue
- ☐ Brown
- z Medium green
- − Dark red
- ▽ Light grey
- ∧ Dark grey
- ★ Pink
- ▲ Orange
- × Dark green
- ● Sand
  Lettering in brown

### Prayer bookmark

- ☐ Brown
- ● Yellow
- ★ Pink
- × Pale green
  Lettering in brown

*N.B. Check the colour numbers given in the requirements list for the exact shades to use for each bookmark*

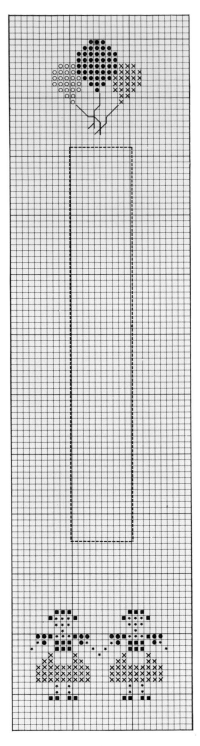

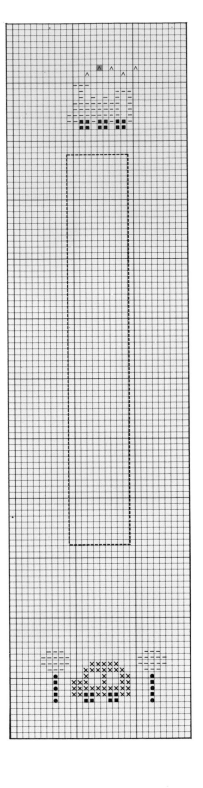

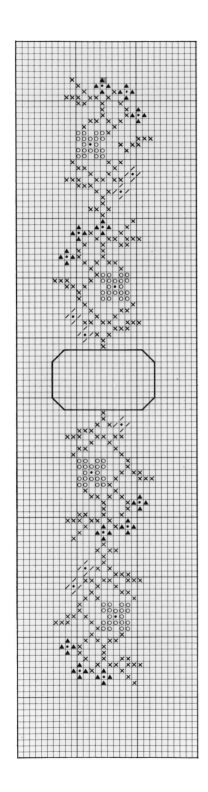

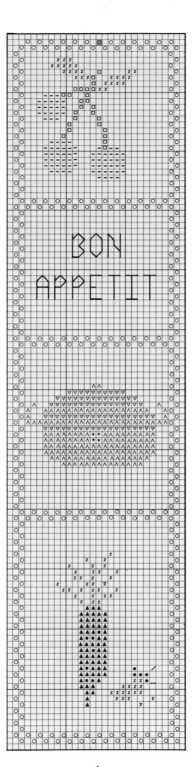

BON

APPETIT

Our
Father
which
art
in
Heaven

# CHRISTMAS CARDS

A project to demonstrate the different effect achieved by altering the count of the fabric. The cards in particular are a simple project and would be suitable for children to work. The five designs are initially worked on a medium count fabric to produce designs of a suitable size for Christmas cards but they can also be stitched on a finer count of fabric to give a much smaller motif to fit gift tags or tree decorations.

## REQUIREMENTS

4 oval card blanks and backing sheets
1 circular card blank and backing sheet
4 pieces of white 14 count Aida fabric: each piece 10 × 12 cm (4 × 5 in)
1 piece of white 14 count Aida, 9 × 9 cm (3½ × 3½ in)
Fabric adhesive
Tapestry needle size 22 or 24

Stranded cottons as follows (one skein of each of the following colours is sufficient to work all the designs):

| Colour | DMC | Anchor |
|--------|-----|--------|
| Red | 666 | 046 |
| Green | 904 | 0258 |
| Black | 310 | 0403 |
| Pink | 605 | 074 |
| Brown | 898 | 0360 |
| Dark green | 935 | 0269 |
| Yellow | 444 | 0291 |

## CONSTRUCTION

Work the designs using two strands of cotton.

In this project, although 14 count fabric is used, the bright colours of the cottons give sufficient coverage with just two strands.

Fold one of the pieces of fabric into four and crease lightly. This will indicate the centre point which corresponds to the centre mark on the charts on page 27. Begin stitching at this point, working the outlines in back or running stitch.

When the design has been completed, trim the edges of the fabric, so that it is slightly smaller than the backing card.

Gently press the design on the reverse side.

1

Using a fabric adhesive and following the manufacturer's instructions, place a little glue around the edge of the cut-out on the inside of the card.

Lay the design on a flat surface, right side up and position the card on top, so that the design appears centrally in the cut-out area (diagram 1). This needs a steady hand and a good eye, so take your time.

Glue the backing sheet to the reverse of the design to enclose it.

## VARIATIONS: GIFT TAGS

| REQUIREMENTS |
| --- |
| 5 pieces of 18 count Aida: each 8 x 8 cm (3 x 3 in)<br>5 gift tag blanks<br>Fabric adhesive<br>Tapestry needle size 24 or 26<br>Stranded cottons as for cards |

## MAKING UP

All of the designs used for the cards will fit onto gift tags when stitched on a finer fabric and using two strands of cotton, except for the two bells. Use the chart of the single bell instead.

Make up the gift tags in the same way as the Christmas cards.

## TREE DECORATIONS

| REQUIREMENTS |
| --- |
| 3 oval frames<br>1 circular frame<br>1 heart-shaped frame<br>5 pieces of 18 count Aida fabric: each 8 × 8 cm (3 × 3 in)<br>Tapestry needle size 24 or 26<br>Stranded cottons as for cards |

## MAKING UP

The same charts could be used as motifs for oval, circular or heart-shaped tree decorations. It is advisable to work the designs on the size of fabric given, then trim them to the size of the decoration on completion. Work the five designs as given for the Christmas cards but following the single bell variation and using two strands of cotton.

To assemble the designs, trim the edges of the acetate, if necessary, until it fits snugly into the mount. Use this as a guide for trimming the Aida fabric. Work carefully, as it is important to get an exact fit.

Place the acetate in the mount, then the needlework and snap in the plastic backing lock. Use a piece of sticky-backed felt at the back for a neat finish.

## STOCKING DECORATIONS

A further variation on this project is to work the designs on a stocking shape to a size suitable for hanging on the tree.

Enlarge the pattern in diagram 2 to twice the size, then cut out two pieces from 18 count Aida fabric.

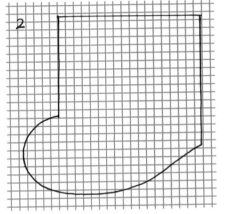

2

Using two strands of cotton, work your chosen design in the foot area of one of the shapes, then place the two pieces right sides together and stitch around the sides, leaving the top open. Turn right side out and press the seams gently. Finish the raw edges at the top with red or green bias binding, forming it into a hanging loop at the back of the stocking (diagram 3).

3

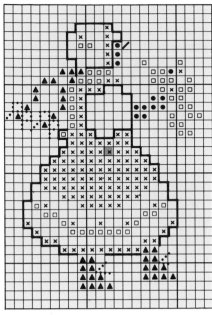

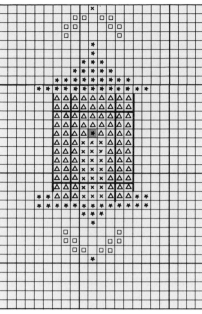

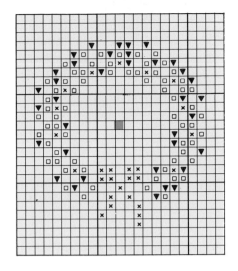

*Above: Girl with holly; Lantern; Wreath. Below: Father Christmas; Bells with single bell variation*

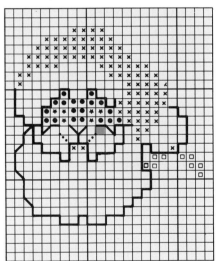

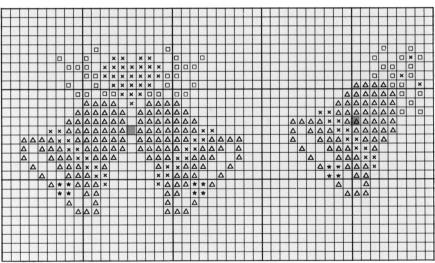

KEY

× Red

▼ Dark green

● Pink

▲ Brown

★ Black

△ Yellow

□ Green

Outline in brown (Girl with holly)
and black (Father Christmas;
Lantern)
Red for moustache (Father Christmas)
and hair ribbons (Girl with holly)

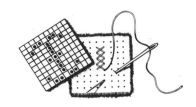

# GREETINGS CARDS

This set of designs provides ideas for cards for special calendar occasions and personalized gift tags for any time of the year. The cards, with the exception of the 'Mother' card, which is worked on a fine count of fabric, are all easy to execute. The designs have been kept simple, both to enable children to participate and to make it possible to stitch the cards at only a few days' notice of the event.

# CONSTRUCTION

Work the designs using two strands of cotton.

With small designs like the gift tags and the simpler cards, mark the centre spot of the design by folding the fabric into four and creasing lightly. This corresponds to the centre mark on the charts on pages 29 and 31. Begin stitching at this point, working the message on the Father's Day card and any line details in back or running stitch. With the remaining designs, tack the centre vertical and horizontal lines as described in the Skill File (page 16).

When the design has been completed, trim the edges of the fabric, so that it is slightly smaller than the corresponding backing card.

Gently press the design on the reverse side.

Mount the design in the card blank following the instructions given on page 25.

## VARIATIONS

The floral alphabet on pages 32 to 33 can be stitched as single initials or combined into names or messages. The samples shown in the photograph are just one or two ideas – the variations are endless.

If you wish to use the alphabet to form a name or word, pencil out the letters on graph paper, leaving one stitch space between each letter. Count the number of squares along the length of the pencilled design, then divide this number in half (see diagram on page 52). Find the centre spot of your fabric and start stitching the design at this point, beginning at the half way point of the name or word and half way up the particular letter.

Other motifs in the following projects can be isolated from the main design and used as designs for special occasion greetings cards. Shown in the photograph on the next page are two such ideas. The 'Baby Congratulations' card features the central motif from the Traditional Birth Sampler on page 58 and the gift tag for a house warming present shows a portion of the heart motif from the Home Sweet Home design (page 34) worked on the same count of fabric.

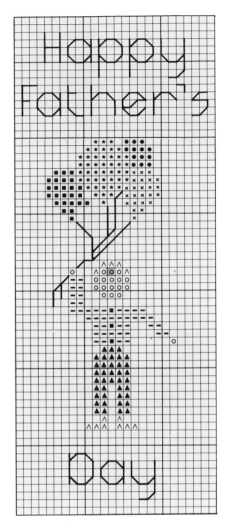

KEY

■ Dark blue
★ Bright yellow
▲ Bright green
× Pink
○ Pale pink
– Yellow
● Green
∧ Brown
 Lettering in dark blue
 Balloon strings in grey
 Mouth in red
 Eyes in brown

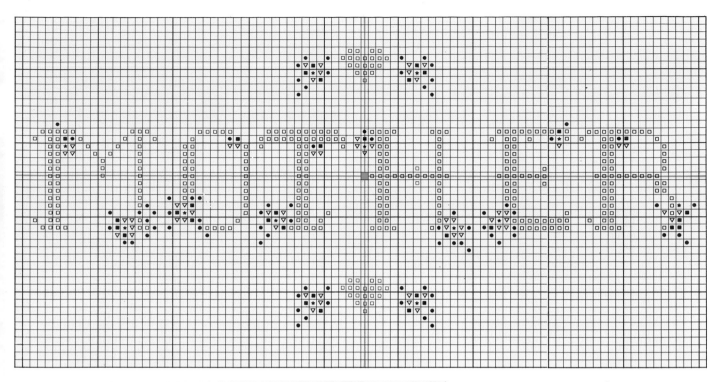

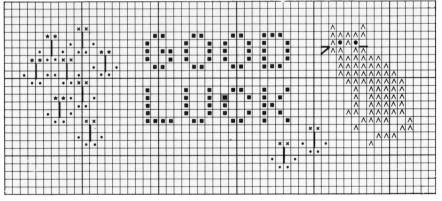

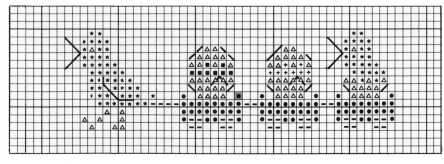

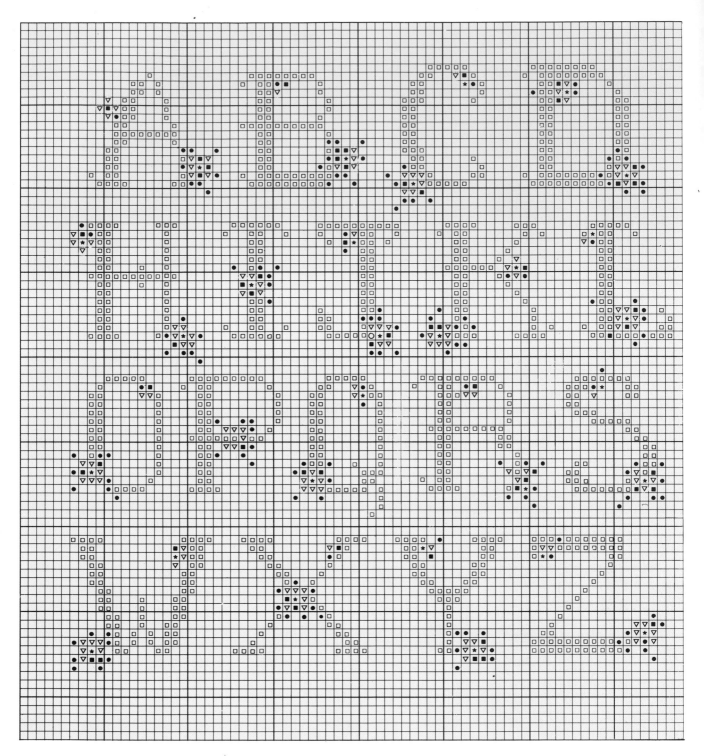

KEY

KEY
□ Pink
• Bright green
■ Dark blue
▽ Light blue
★ Yellow

33

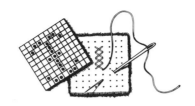

# HOME SWEET HOME

Bright with primary colours, this piece is designed
as a picture to hang in the hallway of your house. The design
does take quite a time to execute as it is heavily filled
in but it is made easier by the fact that most of the colours are
worked in blocks rather than as single stitches.

The placing of the lettering can be changed if you already have a particular frame you wish to mount the work in. The amount of fabric required should also be adjusted to suit the dimensions of the frame with enough extra to wrap round the backing material.

---

### REQUIREMENTS

1 piece of white 18 count Aida fabric, 24 × 18 cm (10 × 7 in): this will fit the frame shown with the actual finished size of the picture measuring 14 × 6 cm (5½ × 2½ in)

Wadding to fit the frame (optional, see page 92)

Tapestry needle size 24 or 26

Stranded cottons as follows:

| Colour | DMC | Anchor |
|---|---|---|
| Blue | 793 | 0121 |
| White | Blanc | White |
| Very dk green | 895 | 0269 |
| Dark green | 367 | 0216 |
| Medium green | 320 | 0215 |
| Light green | 471 | 0265 |
| Brown | 433 | 0358 |
| Red | 666 | 046 |
| Yellow | 307 | 0290 |
| Dark blue | 796 | 0133 |
| Bright green | 702 | 0227 |
| Light brown | 436 | 0363 |
| Pink | 605 | 074 |

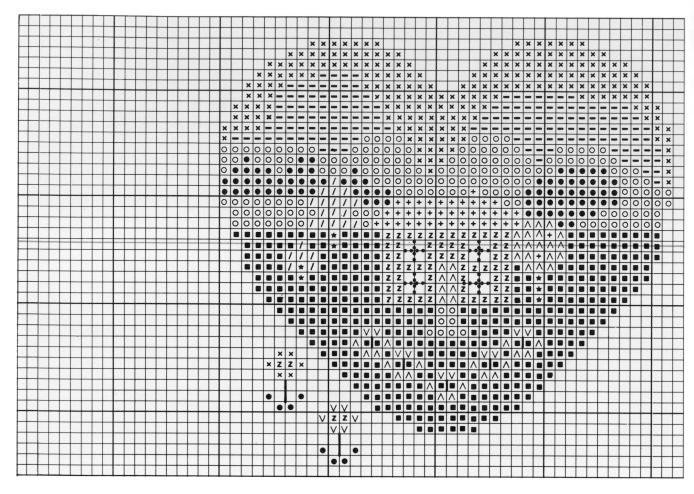

Fold the Aida fabric in half lengthwise and crease lightly to find the centre vertical line. Measure 8 cm (3¼ in) down this line from the top. This is the starting point for the stitching and corresponds to the top centre point on the chart which is split over two pages above and right.

Work the design using two strands of cotton. The dark blue detail near the centre of the heart is worked in back or running stitch.

Gently press the design on the reverse over a padded cloth and mount in the chosen frame.

## VARIATIONS

The same design could be worked for an upright rectangular frame if the lettering were to be positioned below the heart and the two flowers placed above it, one on either side. This would give a finished design measuring 7.5 × 12 cm (3 × 4¾ in).

The heart and flowers motif on its own, if worked on the same count of fabric, would make a good design for the lid of a 7.5 cm (3 in) diameter pot.

The house will just fit into a gift tag blank, as shown in the photograph on page 30.

# CONSTRUCTION

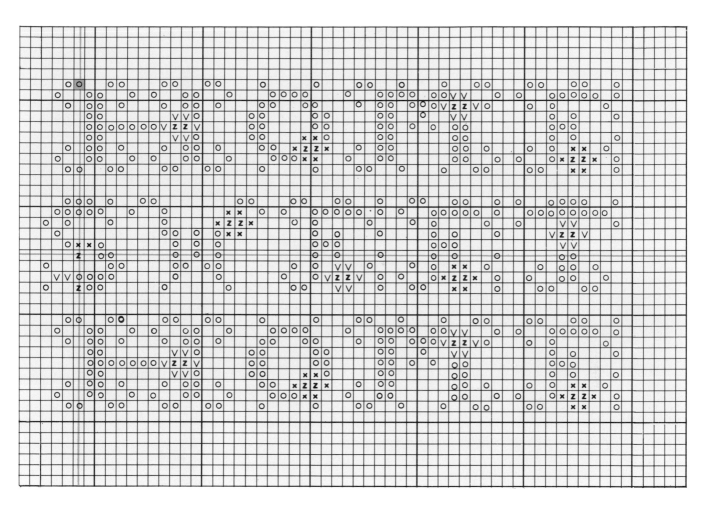

KEY

× Blue
− White
● Medium green
/ Very dark green
○ Dark green
■ Light green
+ Red
z Yellow

∧ Bright green
∨ Pink
★ Brown
⊙ Light brown
••• Windows in dark blue

| Flower stems in medium green

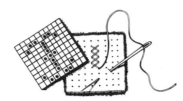

# DRESSING TABLE SET

This design group looks more complicated to stitch
than it actually is. If the colours are not quite right for your bedroom,
change the flower shades to suit your particular colour scheme.

REQUIREMENTS

For the hairbrush: 1 piece of
white 18 count Aida fabric, 12
× 14 cm (5 × 6 in)
For the mirror: 1 piece of white
18 count Aida fabric, 18 ×
18 cm (7 × 7 in)
For the clothes brush: 1 piece of
white 22 count Aida fabric, 9 ×
19 cm (3½ × 7½ in)
Hairbrush, mirror and clothes
brush blanks (page 93)
Iron-on interfacing, same size as
Aida fabrics used
Tapestry needle size 24 or 26
Stranded cottons as follows (one
skein of each will be enough):

| Colour | DMC | Anchor |
|---|---|---|
| Pink | 605 | 074 |
| Dark pink | 223 | 0895 |
| Light green | 471 | 0265 |
| Yellow | 445 | 0288 |
| Green | 988 | 0257 |
| Dark peach | 353 | 08 |
| Light peach | 951 | 0880 |
| Dark blue | 793 | 0121 |
| Light blue | 809 | 0129 |

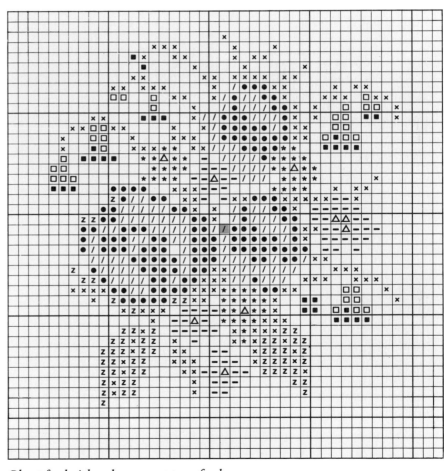

*Chart for hairbrush, see next page for key*

Work the designs for the hairbrush (page 39) and mirror (this page) using two strands of cotton and for the clothes brush (next page) using one strand.

Work each of the designs in the following manner. Begin by tacking the centre vertical and horizontal lines as described in the Skill File (page 16) to establish the centre of the fabric. Commence the stitching at this point, following the corresponding centre stitch as marked on the charts.

When the stitching is completed, make sure the fabric is square, then back with iron-on interfacing.

To assemble the design into the blank hair brush, mirror or clothes brush, follow the manufacturer's instructions, trimming the fabric to fit.

*Chart for mirror, see key below*

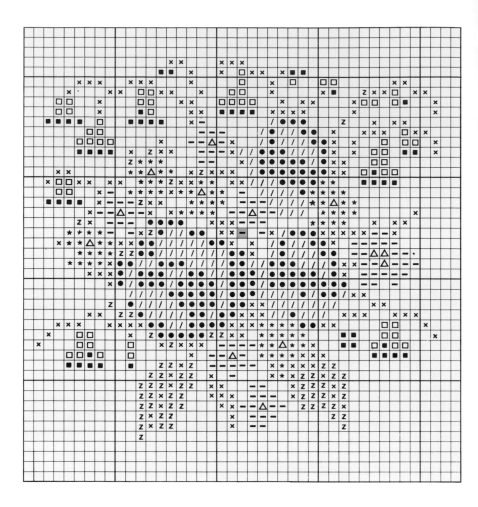

KEY
- ■ Dark peach
- □ Light peach
- × Green
- z Light green
- — Light blue
- ★ Dark blue
- / Dark pink
- ● Pink
- △ Yellow

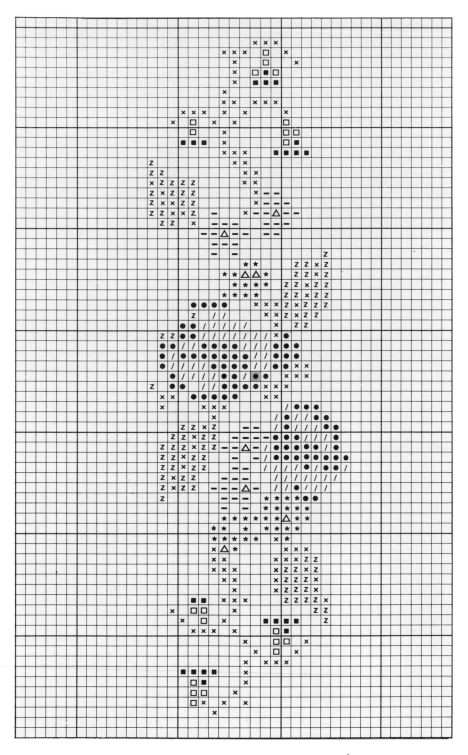

The hairbrush design could also be used to make a lavender or pot pourri bag as a drawer freshener. A small project such as this is also useful for using up left over pieces of fabric and threads.

You will need two pieces of 18 count Aida fabric, 11 × 11 cm (4¼ × 4¼ in).

Stitch the design on one of the pieces, then place the two fabric squares, right sides together. Stitch around three sides, either by hand using back stitch or by machine, leaving a 6 mm (¼ in) seam allowance.

Turn through to the right side, press the seams lightly, then fill with a pot pourri mixture or dried lavender. Slip stitch the remaining sides together and attach a ribbon for a pretty finish.

*Chart for clothes brush, see key opposite*

# BATHROOM ACCESSORIES

This set shows how a simple motif of two flowers can be extended to form three different designs that can be grouped together but will also stand alone most effectively.

For the mirror: 1 piece of cream 18 count Aida fabric, 15 × 18 cm (6 × 7 in)

For the crystal pot: 1 piece of white 18 count Aida fabric, 14 × 14 cm (5½ × 5½ in)

1 Sal-EM handtowel (page 93)
1 mirror blank (page 93)
1 7.5 cm (3 in) diameter crystal pot (page 93)

Iron-on interfacing, same size as Aida fabrics used

Tapestry needle size 24 or 26

Stranded cottons as follows (one skein of each will be enough for all the designs):

| Colour | DMC | Anchor |
|---|---|---|
| Green | 367 | 0216 |
| Light blue | 341 | 0120 |
| Yellow | 445 | 0288 |
| Dark blue | 340 | 0118 |
| Sand | 436 | 0363 |
| Light pink | 605 | 074 |
| Medium pink | 3688 | 066 |
| Dark pink | 961 | 040 |
| Bright blue | 798 | 0131 |

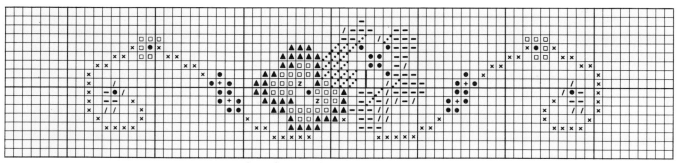

*Chart for towel, see next page for key*

To work the mirror, begin by folding the Aida fabric in half lengthwise and crease lightly to find the centre vertical line. Measure 3 cm (1¼ in) down this line from the top. This is the starting point for the stitching and corresponds to the top centre point on the chart on page 45.

Stitch the designs using two strands of cotton.

When the design is complete, ensure that the fabric is not distorted, then press gently on the reverse over a padded surface. Back with iron-on interfacing, then trim to the size of the frame above the mirror. Place in the mount and seal with the backing provided, following the manufacturer's instructions.

To work the pot, begin by tacking the centre vertical and horizontal lines as described in the Skill File (page 16) to establish the centre of the fabric. Commence the stitching at this point, following the corresponding centre stitch as marked on the chart above.

When the stitching is completed, make sure the fabric is square, then back with iron-on interfacing.

To assemble the design into the crystal pot lid, follow the manufacturer's instructions, trimming the fabric to fit.

To work the handtowel, use two strands of cotton and follow the chart on page 43. Since the 26 count

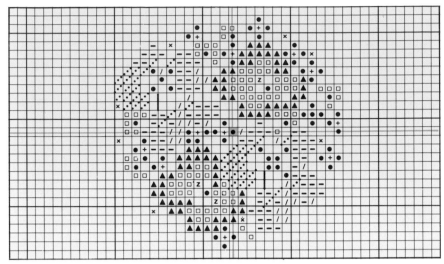

*Chart for pot, see key below*

of this fabric is so fine, work each stitch over two counts or threads, which will give a clearer motif. The motif can be worked once in the middle of the towel, as shown in the photograph on page 42, or as a series across the width.

To position the first motif in the middle of the towel, fold the towel in half vertically, crease lightly and mark this fold with a row of tacking. Count 49 threads up the line of tacking from the bottom of the towel to find the lowest point of the chart, then count up from this point to find the centre stitch as marked on the chart.

To work a series of motifs, fold the towel in half lengthwise to find the central point and begin stitching the first motif at this point (starting with the centre stitch as marked on the chart). Work the motifs to the

**KEY**
/ Light pink
− Medium pink
.˙ Dark pink
▲ Light blue
□ Dark blue
z Bright blue
● Yellow
+ Sand
× Green
Petal detail in yellow

left and right of this point, leaving four stitch spaces between each motif and finishing either with a complete motif or part of one, according to your preference.

If working a towel with an even-weave band, fold the stitching area of the handtowel in half lengthwise, then crosswise to find the centre point. This corresponds to the centre stitch marked on the chart. Begin stitching here.

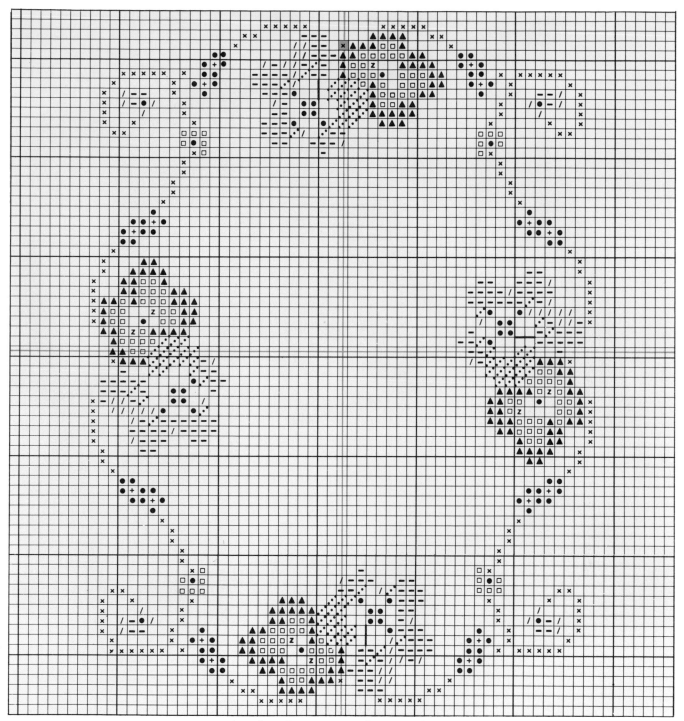

*Chart for mirror, see key opposite*

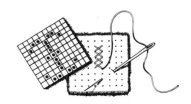

# DESIGN FOR A TRAY

This flower picture has been specially designed to fit
the tray mount shown in the photograph and uses a wide range
of shades to produce a bright and colourful display.
However, if you prefer to stitch one of the other designs,
for example from the four seasons motifs given later, or to create
your own, the instructions provide details on
how to achieve this.

### REQUIREMENTS

1 piece of white 18 count Aida
fabric, 32 × 32 cm (12½ ×
12½ in)
1 tray mount blank (page 93)
Tapestry needle size 24 or 26
Stranded cottons as follows:

| Colour | DMC | Anchor |
| --- | --- | --- |
| Donkey brown | 642 | 0392 |
| Rust | 436 | 0363 |
| Dark brown | 841 | 0378 |
| Dark pink | 335 | 041 |
| Pink | 899 | 027 |
| Light pink | 818 | 024 |
| Light green | 3347 | 0266 |
| Very pale green | 3052 | 0861 |
| Green | 367 | 0216 |
| Dark yellow | 743 | 0305 |
| Light yellow | 744 | 0301 |
| Daffodil gold | 742 | 0303 |
| Chocolate brown | 610 | 0905 |
| Red | 349 | 013 |
| Dark red | 221 | 0896 |
| Acid green | 732 | own choice |
| Yellow | 445 | 0288 |
| Lavender | 553 | 098 |
| Violet | 327 | 0101 |
| Very dark blue | 939 | 0152 |
| Dusky rose | 315 | 0970 |
| Dull dk green | 3051 | 0862 |
| Blue | 809 | 0129 |
| Dark blue | 939 | 0152 |
| Dull green | 3363 | 320 |
| Teasel brown | 642 | 0392 |
| White | Blanc | White |
| Black | 310 | 0403 |

To work the chart opposite, begin by tacking the centre vertical and horizontal lines as described in the Skill File (page 16) to establish the centre of the fabric. Commence the stitching at this point, following the corresponding centre stitch as marked on the chart and working back or running stitch for the fine lines on the tulip, mistletoe and teasel.

Work the design using two strands of cotton.

*N.B. You will find that some of the shades used here have been used in previous projects but have been given a different symbol. This has been done to give a better definition to the shapes, so as to make the chart easier to follow.*

When the stitching is completed, press gently on the reverse over a padded cloth, then assemble in the tray mount, following the manufacturer's instructions.

To create your own design for a circular piece, it is aesthetically pleasing to echo the shape of the mount, as in the design shown.

To achieve this, after the centre horizontal and vertical lines have been tacked, fold the cloth from corner to corner, crease lightly and tack the diagonal line thus formed. Repeat for the second diagonal.

Next, mark with a single stitch the point at which the edge of the mount, when placed centrally on the fabric, crosses each of the tacked lines. Count an equal number of stitches down each line to allow a margin all round. Mark with tacking stitches (diagram 1).

Now count the number of threads along the centre vertical line in the design area. Count and mark off in pencil the same number on a piece of graph paper both vertically and horizontally. This gives you the

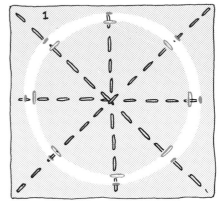

broad outlines of your design area. Remember, however, that the scale of the graph paper will probably not be the same as the finished piece. See the Skill File on page 92 for further information on creating designs on graph paper.

KEY

▽ Daffodil gold
∕ Light yellow
⚡ Dark yellow
z Light green
× Green
− Rust
+ Donkey brown
▲ Chocolate brown
● Pink
D Dark pink
⊙ Light pink
○ Teasel brown
▼ Red
• Dark red
Ø Black

S Very dark blue
∧ Dusky rose
⊡ Very pale green
★ Yellow
⊕ Blue
Ⅰ Dark blue
■ Dull green
△ Dark brown
□ Acid green
W White
∵ Dull dark green
L Lavender
∨ Violet

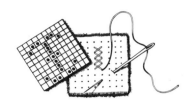

# MODERN SAMPLER FOR A NEW BABY

Of the three sampler projects, this is the easiest to sew,
as it is stitched on a larger count of fabric. It has been worked in two
colourways, one bright, the other pastel, to suit the particular
colour scheme of the nursery.

### REQUIREMENTS

1 piece of white 14 count Aida fabric, 35 × 26 cm (14 × 10½ in)
Tapestry needle size 22 or 24
Stranded cottons as follows:

**Primary colourway**

| Colour | DMC | Anchor |
|---|---|---|
| Blue | 312 | 0979 |
| Brown | 801 | 0359 |
| Bright green | 702 | 0227 |
| Bright yellow | 307 | 0290 |
| Pale yellow | 445 | 0288 |
| Red | 816 | 043 |
| Mauve | 553 | 098 |
| Grey | 317 | 0400 |
| Pink | 605 | 074 |
| Green | 320 | 0215 |
| Dull blue | 793 | 0121 |
| Dark green | 895 | 0269 |

**Pastel colourway**

| Colour | DMC | Anchor |
|---|---|---|
| Pale blue | 813 | 0160 |
| Pale brown | 613 | 0853 |
| Pale green | 954 | 0204 |
| Pale yellow | 727 | 0293 |
| Palest yellow | 445 | 0288 |
| Pink | 3688 | 066 |
| Lavender | 210 | 0109 |
| Pale grey | 318 | 0398 |
| Pale pink | 605 | 074 |
| Green | 320 | 0215 |
| Palest blue | 827 | 0159 |
| Medium green | 3347 | 0266 |

Fold the Aida fabric in half lengthwise and crease lightly to find the centre vertical line. Measure 9 cm (3½ in) down this line from the top. This is the starting point for the stitching and corresponds to the top centre point on the chart which is split over pages 56 and 57.

Work the design using 3 strands of cotton.

Stitch the motifs first, using running or back stitch for the cloud, sun rays, boat masts and birds, then stitch the border, leaving the lettering until last. To work out the spacing for the particular names you have chosen, for each line of lettering work as follows.

It is easiest to work out this sequence on graph paper but it can be done without. Write out the names in capital letters, following the alphabet chart opposite, and

spaces between words.

Divide this number in half and mark the point on the graph paper (diagram 1). This corresponds to the centre vertical line on the sampler chart. Begin stitching the centre letter at the corresponding point on your sampler fabric. Work the rest of the letters first to the left of this point, then to the right (or vice versa if you prefer). Work out the date in the same manner.

When the stitching is complete, gently press the design on the reverse over a padded cloth and mount in a frame (page 92). The size of the finished design is 13.5 × 22 cm (5¼ × 8¾ in).

### Variation

Any of the motifs decorating this sampler could be used to stitch a matching design on the baby's bib.

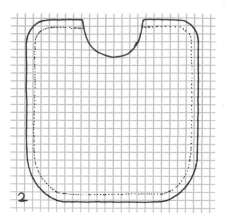

leaving the neck open. Turn right side out and finish the neck with bias binding extended at both ends to form ties. Alternatively, you could use a purchased bib of suitable fabric. Towelling fabric is difficult to use, as it does not provide an instant grid for the stitches. If using, work the design in four strands of cotton, otherwise the stitches may get lost in the pile of the fabric.

Outline the bib area on a piece of graph paper, remembering that the scale of the paper may differ from the count of the fabric, then transfer any of the motifs you would like to stitch from the sampler. It could be a group of motifs, such as the boats at the bottom, a repeat of one motif, e.g. a row of balloons or a single motif, such as the sun and clouds at the top of the sampler.

Various different groupings are shown in the charts on page 55. Shown there also are ideas for combining names with the motifs to make a personalized bib.

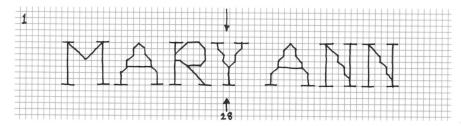

leaving one square (representing one stitch space) between each letter. Count the number of horizontal stitches in each of the letters of the name, including the one stitch spacing between each. If more than one word is to be worked on the same line, allow three stitch

The bib can be made up using 14 count Aida fabric and following the design in diagram 2, enlarged to 23 cm (9 in) across, including a 1.5 cm (⅝) seam allowance all around. Cut two pieces and work the design on one of them, then join, right sides together, and stitch,

ABCDEFGHIJK
LMNOPQRST
UVWXYZ

abcdefghijklmn
opqrstuvwxyz

1234567890

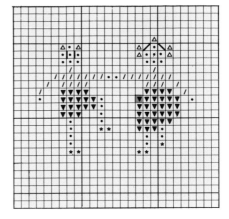

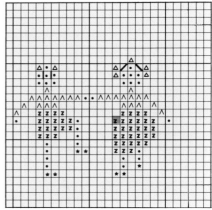

Two colourways for playing
children: the two charts can be
joined in a row

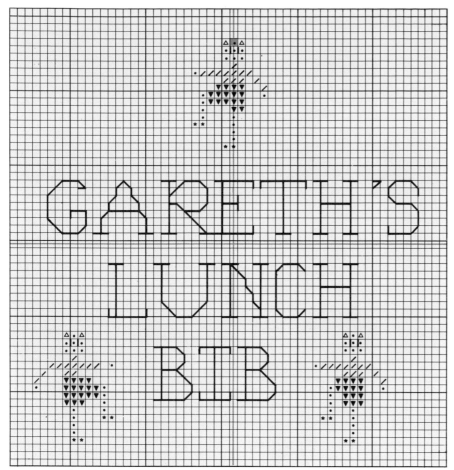

A personalized bib design using the lettering on page 53

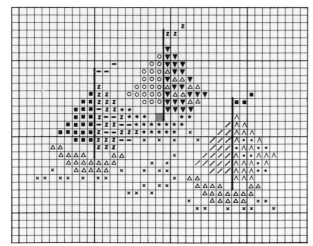

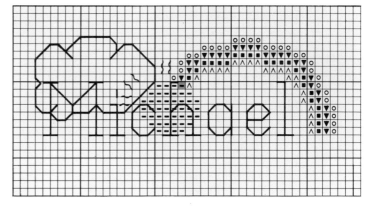

Left: a regrouping of the yachts. Above: adding a child's name
using the lettering on page 53

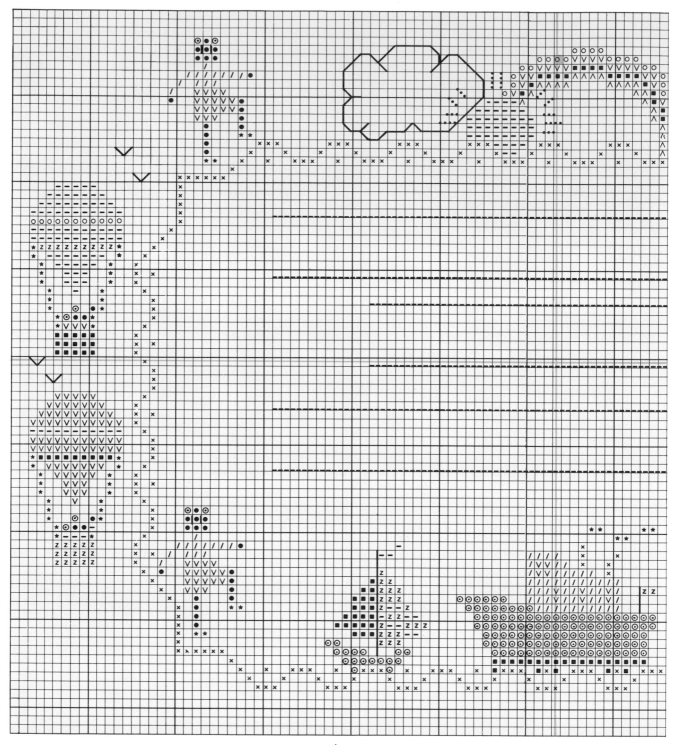

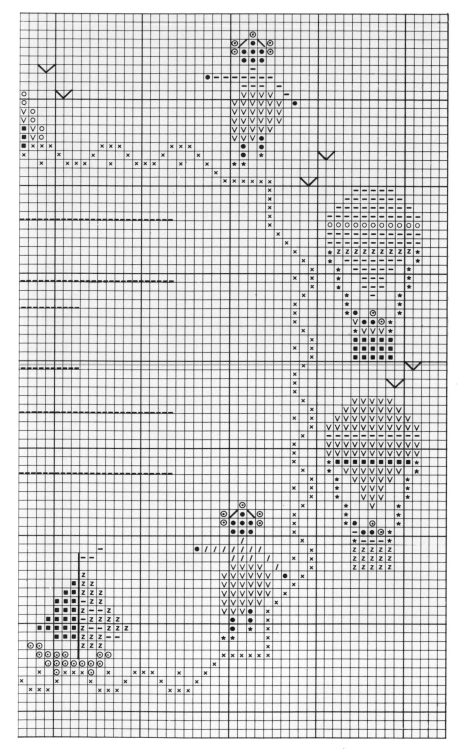

**KEYS**

*Primary colourway*

| | |
|---|---|
| × | Blue |
| ⊙ | Brown |
| z | Bright green |
| — | Bright yellow |
| / | Pale yellow |
| ■ | Red |
| V | Mauve |
| ★ | Grey |
| ● | Pink |
| ∧ | Green |
| ○ | Dull blue |

Date of birth in dark green
Name in red
Cloud in blue
Sunbeams in bright yellow
Birds and boat masts in brown

*Pastel colourway*

| | |
|---|---|
| × | Pale blue |
| ⊙ | Pale brown |
| z | Pale green |
| — | Pale yellow |
| / | Palest yellow |
| ■ | Pink |
| V | Lavender |
| ★ | Pale grey |
| ● | Pale pink |
| ∧ | Green |
| ○ | Palest blue |

Date of birth in medium green
Name in pink
Cloud in pale blue
Sunbeams in pale yellow
Birds and boat masts in pale brown

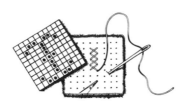

# TRADITIONAL BIRTH SAMPLER

This design follows the traditional Victorian idea of a sampler and is worked in antique shades. It includes the tree of life motif, which Victorian and Edwardian samplers contained to wish the newborn baby longevity. Instructions are given for making a unique sampler to relate to a particular family, by working different permutations of the family group shown and by adding your own motifs.

## CONSTRUCTION

Fold the Aida fabric in half lengthwise and crease lightly to find the centre vertical line. Tack, then measure 6 cm (2½ in) down this line from the top. This is the starting point for the stitching and corresponds to the top centre point on the chart which is divided over pages 62 to 65.

Work the design using 2 strands of cotton.

Stitch the border design and the tree of life following the chart, working the tendrils in back or running stitch.

To personalize the sampler, work as follows:

### Name and date of birth

Count the number of horizontal stitches in the letters of the name or names you wish to include, following the alphabet design given in the chart on page 61. Add one stitch space between each letter. If more than one word is to be worked on the same line, add three stitch spaces between each name.

If the child's first names are quite short, you many wish to place them both on the top line and add the surname below. Four vertical stitch spaces are left between the lines.

*N.B. Working this out on graph paper makes the spacing clearer and*

*will give you an individual stitch guide.*

Divide the total number of stitches in each line by half and count along the horizontal stitches of the letters in the names until you reach this point, remembering to count the one stitch spaces between each letter (see diagram on page 52). Line up this centre stitch with the tacked centre vertical line on the sampler. Begin to work the name at this point, working either to the left or to the right, whichever you prefer.

## Family group
Here, too, there is scope for personalizing your sampler. The photograph and chart show a family group of two adults, a boy, a girl and the baby in a crib, thus showing

that the newborn baby to whom this sampler is dedicated is the third child in the family. If the child is the first, then omit the other two children. If the child is the second, then leave out either the boy or girl as appropriate.

Remember to recentralize this group of figures if your changes have unbalanced the design.

## Family interests
Once the main details of the sampler have been worked, you could add some extra motifs to indicate favourite pets or individual hobbies. As an example, the chart below shows a cat and a dog as well as a motif to indicate a gardening enthusiast. Place these or designs of your own making wherever you

wish within the border but so that the balance of the design is maintained.

## Initials
Finally, use the smaller alphabet chart below to add the initials of either the parents, the whole family or yourself.

The variations are endless, so that each sampler worked will be a celebration of an individual newborn child, as well as a pictorial history of the family and their interests, as recorded at the time of the birth of that child.

When the stitching is complete, gently press the design on the reverse over a padded surface and mount in a frame (page 92).

KEY
● Green
▲ Blue
○ Dark pink
★ Light green
∨ Pink
/ Rust
× Brown

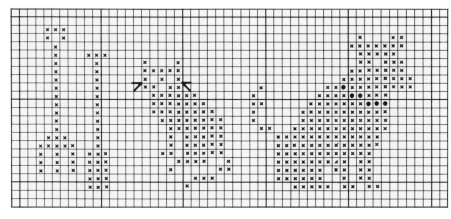

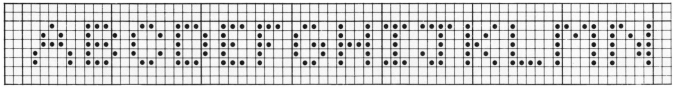

*Top: family interest motif ideas. Above: small alphabet chart for initials*

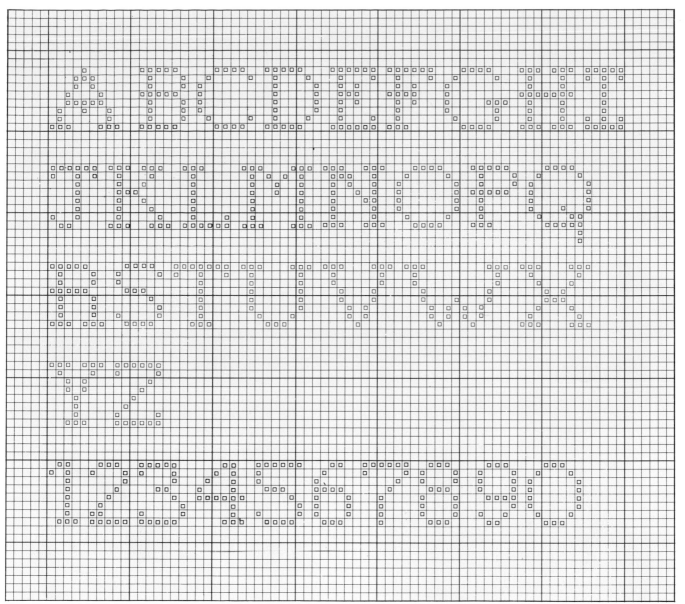

*Chart for child's name and date of birth*

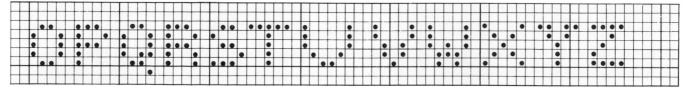

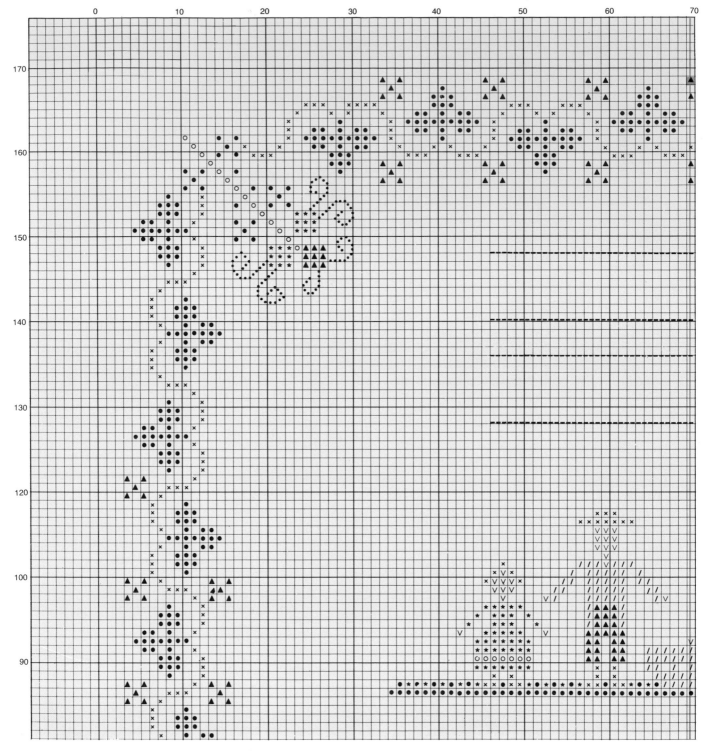

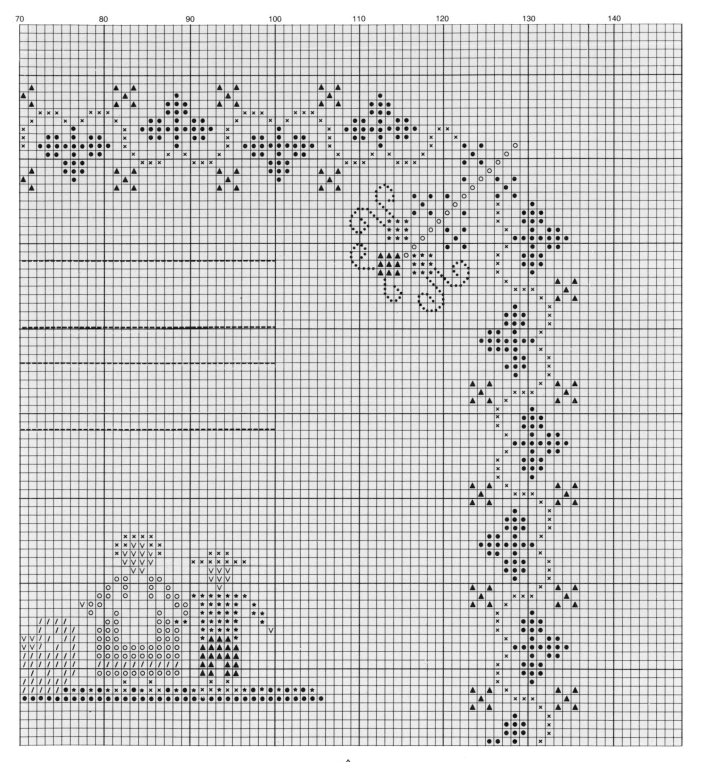

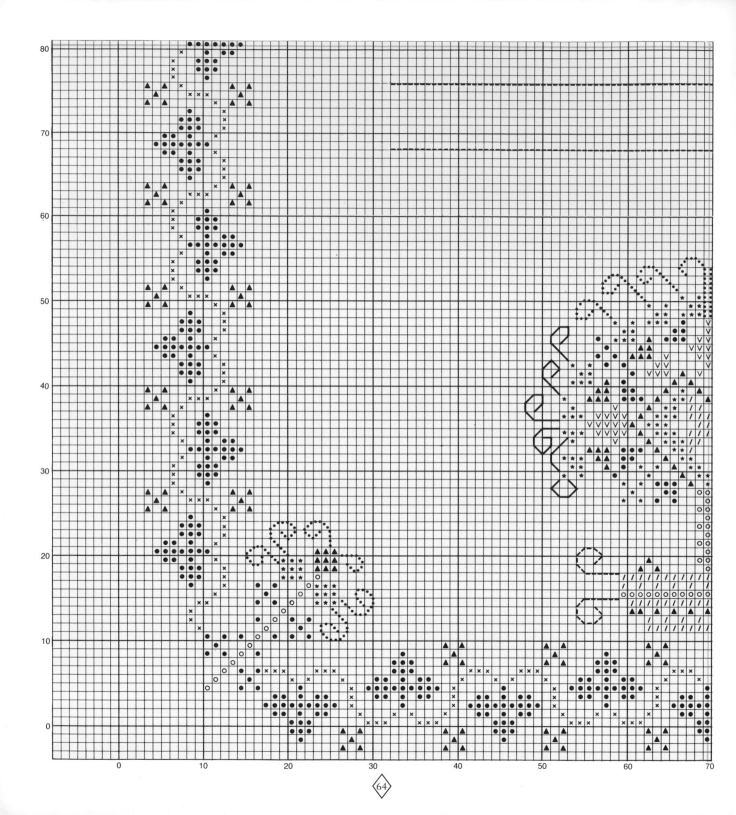

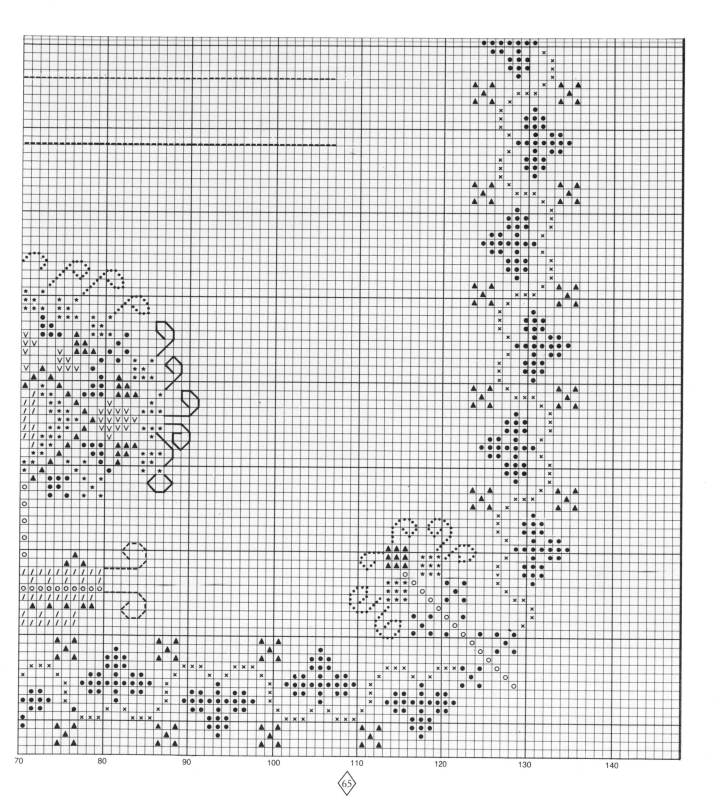

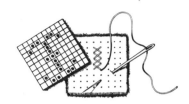

# WEDDING SAMPLER

A quotation from Robert Browning provides an appropriate text for this wedding sampler. Variations are suggested in the instructions to make this suitable either for the marriage itself or for a silver or golden anniversary.

## REQUIREMENTS

1 piece of white or cream 18 count Aida fabric, 33 × 30 cm (13 × 12 in)
Tapestry needle size 24 or 26
Stranded cottons as follows:

| Colour | DMC | Anchor |
|--------|-----|--------|
| Bright blue | 334 | 0977 |
| Light pink | 605 | 074 |
| Light blue | 827 | 0159 |
| Dark grey | 317 | 0400 |
| Yellow | 445 | 0288 |
| Dark pink | 335 | 041 |
| Green | 3363 | 320 |
| Light grey | 318 | 0398 |

Gold or silver (if working an anniversary version)

## CONSTRUCTION

Stitch the design using two strands of cotton.

Begin by tacking the centre vertical and horizontal lines as described in the Skill File (page 16) to establish the centre of the fabric. Measure 6 cm (2½ in) down from the top of the vertical line, this will give the position of the top centre stitch as marked on the chart on page 69.

Work the border design, except for the bells in the top two corners, the church, the bride and the groom in cross stitch. Next work the quotation in back or running stitch.

To make a sampler to celebrate the marriage itself, stitch the wedding date and the bell corner motifs in yellow thread, positioning the date centrally under the church to replace the hearts given in the chart. Instead of the dates on either side of the hearts, you could work a row of the little flowers on either side of the church or some hearts or a mixture of both.

If the sampler is to celebrate a particular anniversary, work as in the photograph, using either gold or silver thread for the relevant celebration. Refer to the chart on pages 72 and 73 for the spacing of the dates in relation to the border and work inwards from the border.

To work the names of the couple, follow the instructions given for the Modern Sampler on page 52, but use the alphabet design given in the chart on page 71.

When the stitching is complete, gently press the design on the reverse over a padded surface and mount in a frame (page 92).

N.B. The actual finished size of the stitched area is 22 × 19 cm (8³/₄ × 7¹/₂ in).

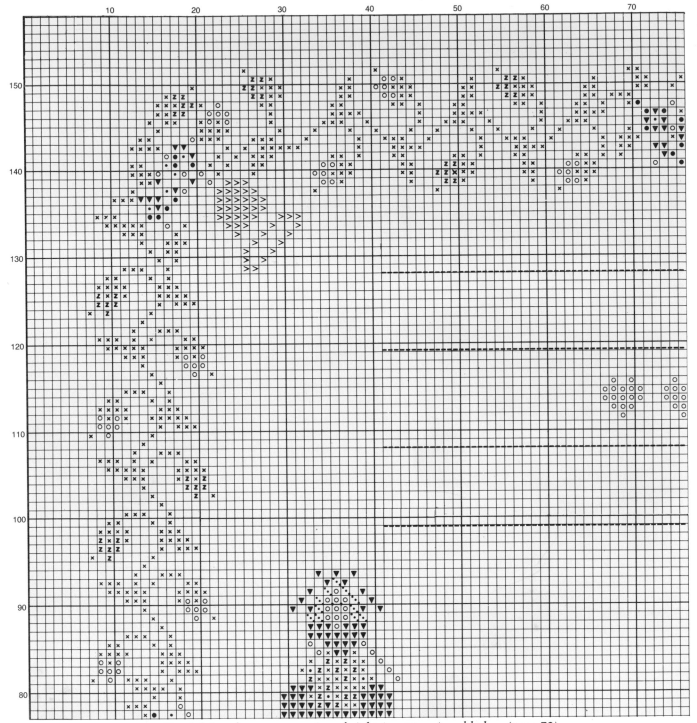

*Top left hand quarter, continued right (next page) and below (page 72)*

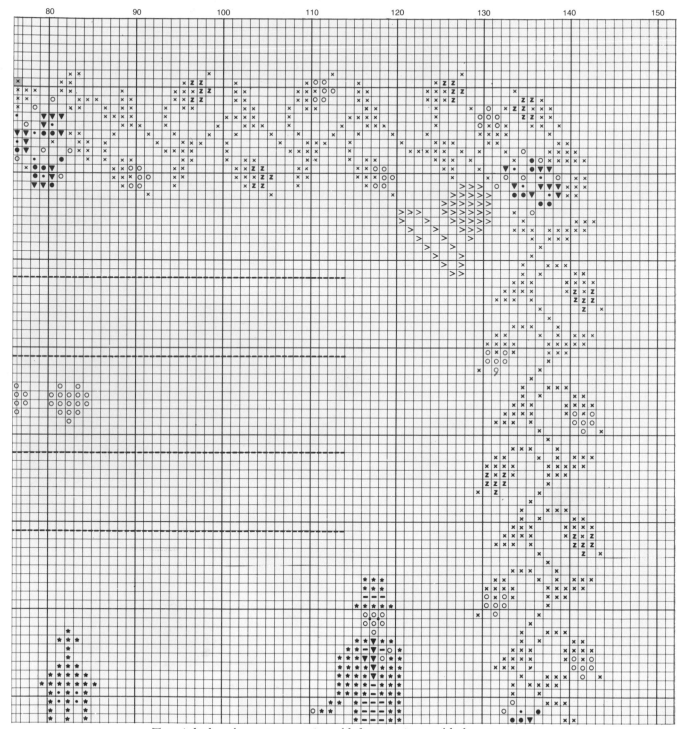

*Top right hand quarter, continued left (opposite) and below (page 73)*

POT

<table>
<tr><td colspan="1" align="center">REQUIREMENTS</td></tr>
</table>

REQUIREMENTS

1 piece of white or cream 18
count Aida fabric, 11 ×
11 cm (4¼ × 4¼ in)
Tapestry needle size 24 or
26
Iron-on interfacing, same
size as Aida fabric
1 × 7.5 or 10 cm (3 or 4 in)
diameter porcelain or
crystal pot (page 93)
Stranded cottons as given
for the wedding sampler
above

MAKING UP

It is possible to use any of the
motifs on the sampler chart as a
design for a 7.5 or 10 cm (3 or 4 in)
pot lid, as shown in the photograph,
where the bride and groom have
been linked and dates given
underneath as a commemoration of
a golden wedding anniversary.

To do this, simply transfer
whichever motif or group of motifs
you choose onto graph paper, then
find the centre horizontal and
vertical lines, which will in turn give
the centre point of the motif. Fold
the Aida fabric in four and crease
lightly to find the centre point.
Begin stitching the centre stitch of
the motif at this point.

Work the design using two strands
of cotton.

When the stitching is completed,
make sure the fabric is square, then

back with iron-on interfacing.

To assemble the design into the pot
lid, follow the manufacturer's
instructions, having trimmed the
fabric to fit.

**Greetings card**
The central motifs would also work
well for a wedding congratulations
card. Refer to the Christmas Cards
project for further details.

KEY
● Bright blue
○ Light pink
▼ Light blue
* Dark grey
• Yellow
z Dark pink
× Green
– Light grey
> Gold or silver
  Lettering in bright blue

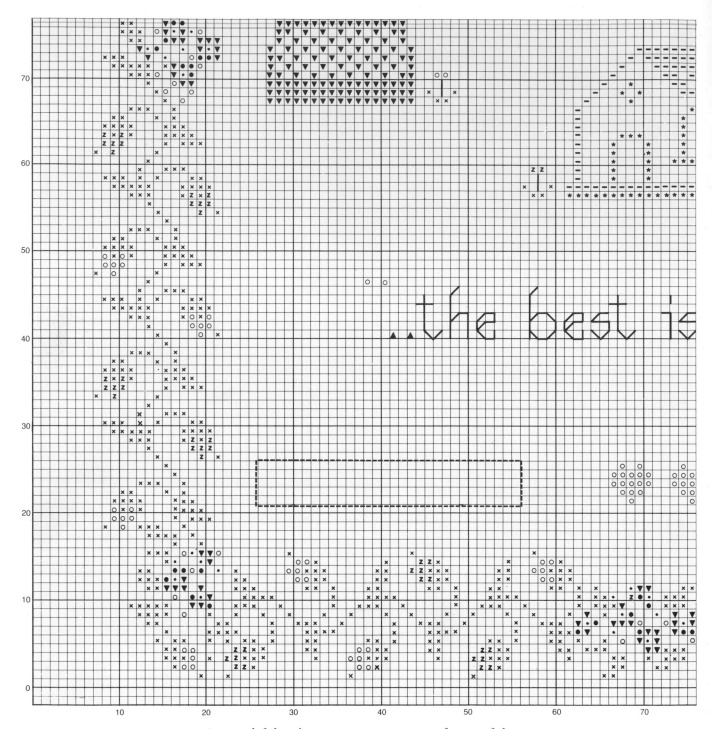

...the best is

# SPRING AND SUMMER PICTURES

Two posies of seasonal flowers which can be worked
singly or grouped together as a pair. They could also be worked
into one large project with the Autumn and Winter designs
which follow. The designs are quite complex and should be attempted
only by a fairly experienced needlewoman.

## REQUIREMENTS

2 pieces of cream 18 count Aida fabric: each 33 × 27 cm (13 × 10¾ in)
Wadding to fit the frames (optional, see page 92)
Tapestry needle size 24 or 26
Stranded cottons as follows:

| Colour | DMC | Anchor |
|---|---|---|
| **Spring** | | |
| Light green | 3347 | 0266 |
| V. light green | 3052 | 0861 |
| Summer green | 988 | 0257 |
| Lavender | 209 | 0110 |
| Purple | 550 | 0101 |
| Green | 367 | 0216 |
| Rose pink | 899 | 027 |
| Pale pink | 776 | 025 |
| Dark pink | 335 | 041 |
| V. pale pink | 818 | 024 |
| Pale yellow | 445 | 0288 |

| Colour | DMC | Anchor |
|---|---|---|
| Pale gold | 744* | 0301 |
| Medium yellow | 743 | 0305 |
| Gold | 742 | 0303 |
| Yellow | 744* | 0301 |
| Light blue | 809 | 0129 |
| Dark blue | 793 | 0121 |
| Pale lavender | 211 | 0108 |
| V. pale yellow | 727 | 0293 |
| Lilac | 210 | 0109 |
| Black | 310 | 0403 |

\* N.B. Pale gold and yellow both have the same number.

| Colour | DMC | Anchor |
|---|---|---|
| **Summer** | | |
| Light green | 3347 | 0266 |
| Green | 367 | 0216 |
| Light rose | 3350 | 078 |
| Brown | 610 | 0905 |
| Red | 349 | 013 |
| Dark red | 221 | 0896 |
| Black | 310 | 0403 |

| Colour | DMC | Anchor |
|---|---|---|
| Dark green | 3051 | 0862 |
| Burgundy | 315 | 0970 |
| Medium pink | 3354 | 075 |
| Rose | 3350 | 078 |
| Medium green | 988 | 0257 |
| Dark blue | 793 | 0121 |
| Light blue | 809 | 0129 |
| Light peach | 948 | 0933 |
| Dark peach | 352 | 09 |
| Medium peach | 754 | 4146 |
| Peach | 353 | 08 |
| Bright yellow | 445 | 0288 |
| Gold | 972 | 0298 |
| Pink | 894 | 026 |
| Light pink | 963 | 048 |
| Dark dull green | 3052 | 0861 |
| Acid green | 732 | own choice |
| Rust | 436 | 0363 |
| Med. bright pink | 956 | 054 |

The designs are stitched using two strands of cotton.

To work each design separately, begin by tacking the centre vertical and horizontal lines as described in the Skill File (page 16) to establish the centre of the fabric. Commence the stitching at this point, following the corresponding centre stitch as

marked on the relevant chart (pages 76 to 79). Work the stamens (Spring) and the defining lines (Summer) in back or running stitch.

To work the designs as a pair, decide visually how many stitch spaces to leave between each design and work out the amount of fabric needed accordingly. Find the centre

point of the new design and count from this point to the centre point of either chart. Begin stitching at one of these points.

Press gently on the reverse over a padded surface with a steam iron or if necessary rinse gently in warm, soapy water and mount in a frame (page 92).

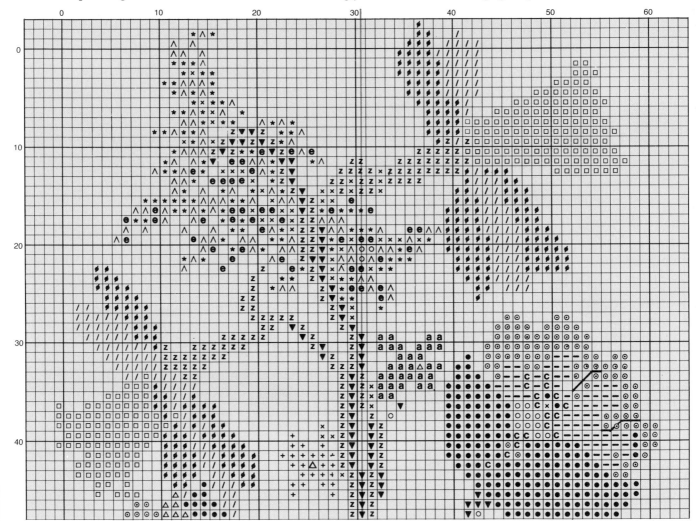

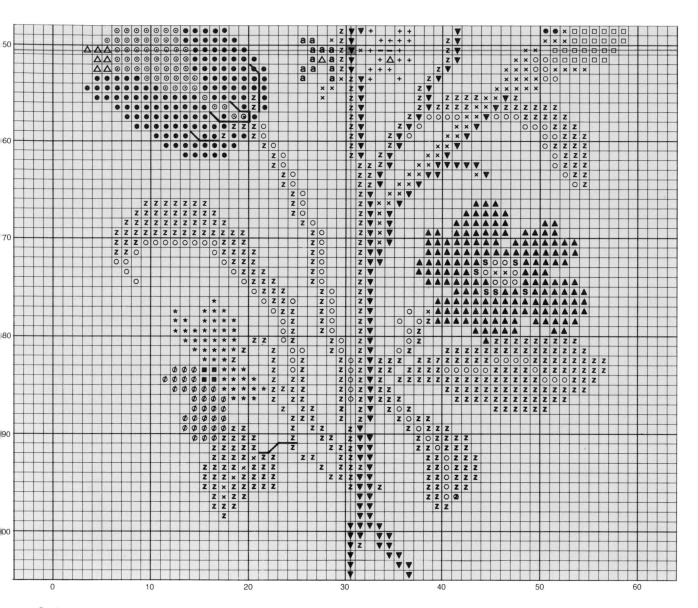

## Spring

- **z** Light green
- **o** V. light green
- **▼** Summer green
- **★** Lavender
- **Ø** Purple
- **×** Green
- **●** Rose pink
- **⊙** Pale pink

- **△** Dark pink
- **−** V. pale pink
- **▲** Pale yellow
- **S** Pale gold
- **✦** Medium yellow
- **□** Gold
- **/** Yellow
- **+** Light blue

- **a** Dark blue
- **∧** Pale lavender
- **■** V. pale yellow
- **e** Lilac
- **C** Black
- Outlines in light green

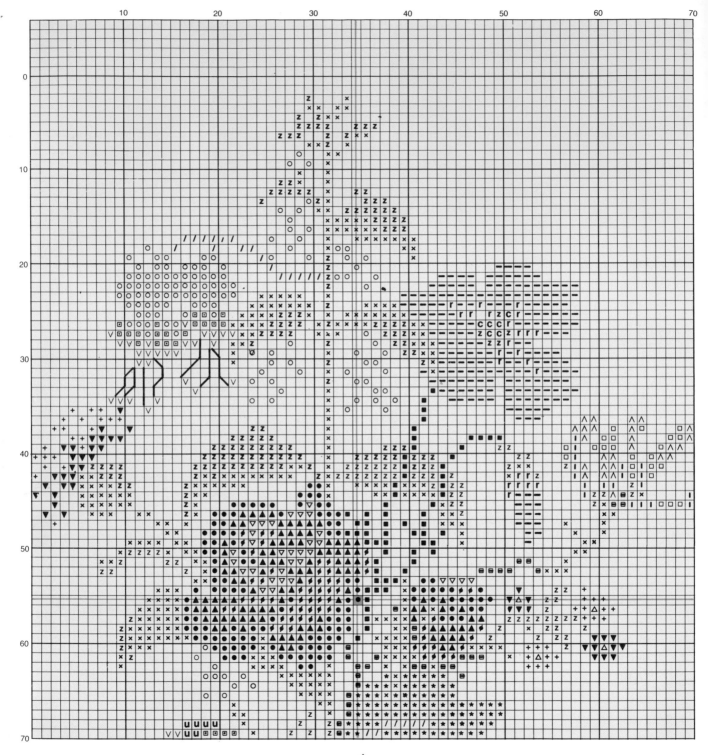

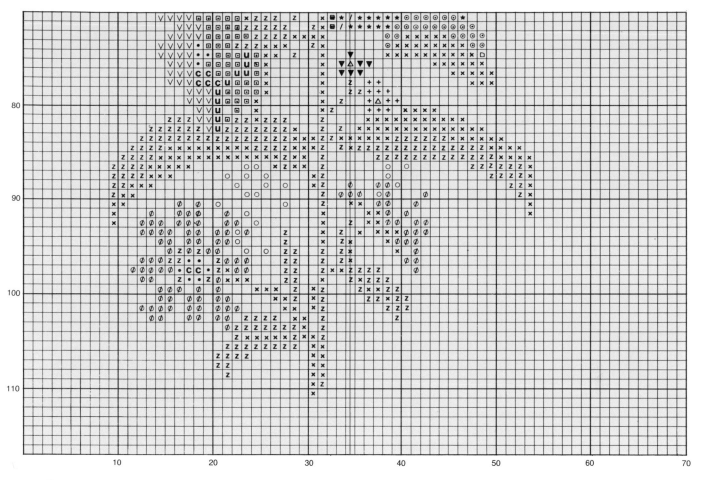

*Summer*

| | | |
|---|---|---|
| z Light green | □ Rose | V Pink |
| Green | ⊟ Medium green | ▣ Light pink |
| o Light rose | ▼ Dark blue | ★ Dark dull green |
| / Brown | + Light blue | ☉ Acid green |
| — Red | ● Light peach | • Rust |
| r Dark red | ⚡ Dark peach | u Medium bright pink |
| c Black | ▲ Medium peach | Flower stamens in light green |
| ■ Dark green | ▽ Peach | |
| ∧ Burgundy | △ Bright yellow | |
| I Medium pink | ⌀ Gold | |

# Autumn and Winter Pictures

Two further posies of flowers and berries. As with the Spring and Summer pictures, these can be worked singly, in pairs or as one wonderful group, representing the four seasons.

### Requirements

2 pieces of cream 18 count Aida fabric: each 33 × 27 cm (13 × 10¾ in)

Wadding to fit the frames (optional, see page 92)

Tapestry needle size 24 or 26

Stranded cottons as follows:

| Colour | DMC | Anchor |
|---|---|---|
| **Autumn** | | |
| Donkey brown | 642 | 0392 |
| Rust | 436 | 0363 |
| Dark brown | 610 | 0905 |
| Chocolate brown | 433 | 0358 |
| Green | 367 | 0216 |
| Light green | 3347 | 0266 |
| Dark green | 895 | 0269 |
| Dark blue | 939 | 0152 |
| Dark rose | 315 | 0970 |
| Acid green | 732 | own choice |
| Pink | 223 | 0895 |
| White | blanc | white |
| Dark rust | 301 | 0349 |
| Dull green | 3052 | 0861 |
| Red | 349 | 013 |
| Dark red | 221 | 0896 |
| Lilac | 553 | 098 |
| Purple | 327 | 0101 |
| **Winter** | | |
| Rust | 436 | 0363 |
| Yellow | 445 | 0288 |
| Brown | 610 | 0905 |
| Dark green | 895 | 0269 |
| Dark red | 347 | 019 |
| Bright red | 666 | 046 |
| Pink | 223 | 0895 |
| Black | 310 | 0403 |
| Yellow sand | 783 | 0306 |
| Light green | 3347 | 0266 |
| White | blanc | white |
| Green | 367 | 0216 |
| Dull lt green | 3052 | 0861 |
| Dull dk green | 3051 | 0862 |
| Mink brown | 841 | 0378 |
| Chocolate brown | 433 | 0358 |

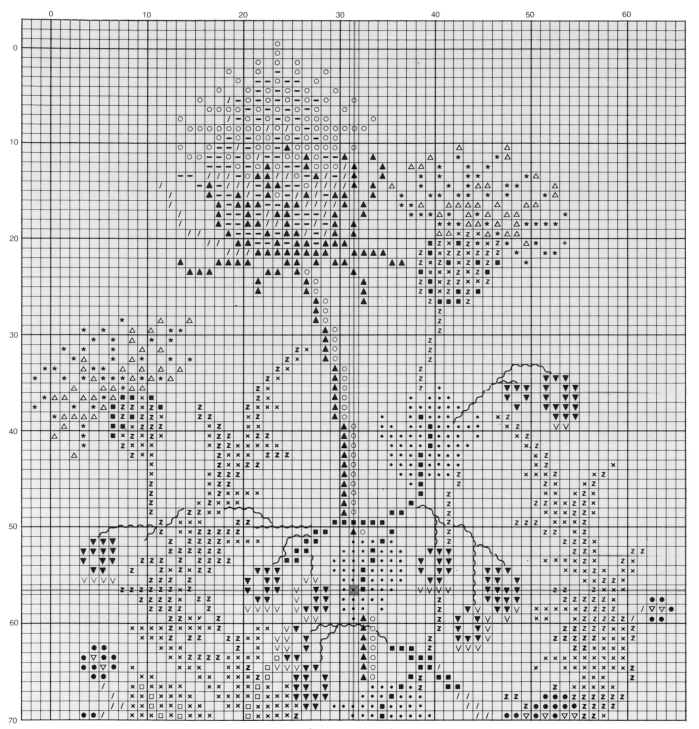

*Autumn chart, continued on page 82*

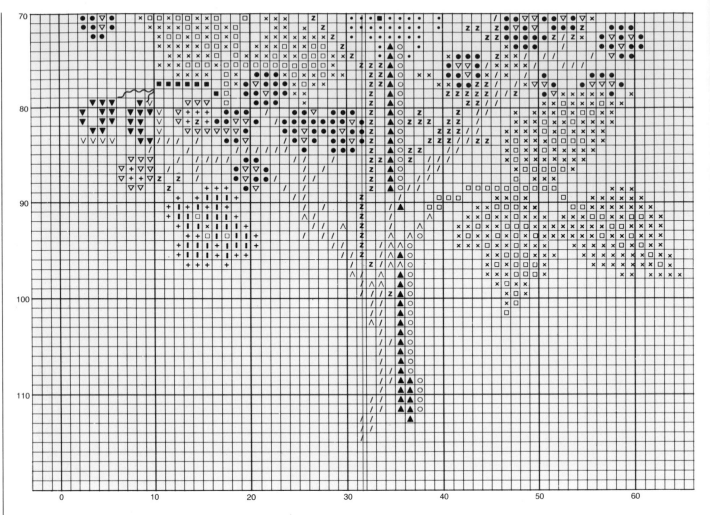

## CONSTRUCTION

Stitch the designs as shown in the charts on pages 81 to 82 for Autumn and 84 to 85 for Winter. Use two strands of cotton and follow the instructions given with the Spring and Summer pictures, working the stems (Autumn) and the yew tree needles, berry outlines and the dried flower (Winter) in running or back stitch. Mount the pictures either in oval frames or in rectangular frames with oval mounts.

### Autumn

| Symbol | Colour | Symbol | Colour |
|---|---|---|---|
| o | Donkey brown | + | Pink |
| – | Rust | I | White |
| ▲ | Dark brown | ∧ | Dark rust |
| / | Chocolate brown | • | Dull green |
| × | Green | ▼ | Red |
| z | Light green | V | Dark red |
| ■ | Dark green | ★ | Lilac |
| ● | Dark blue | △ | Purple |
| ▽ | Dark rose | | Flower stalks in dark green |
| □ | Acid green | | |

*Winter chart, continued next page*

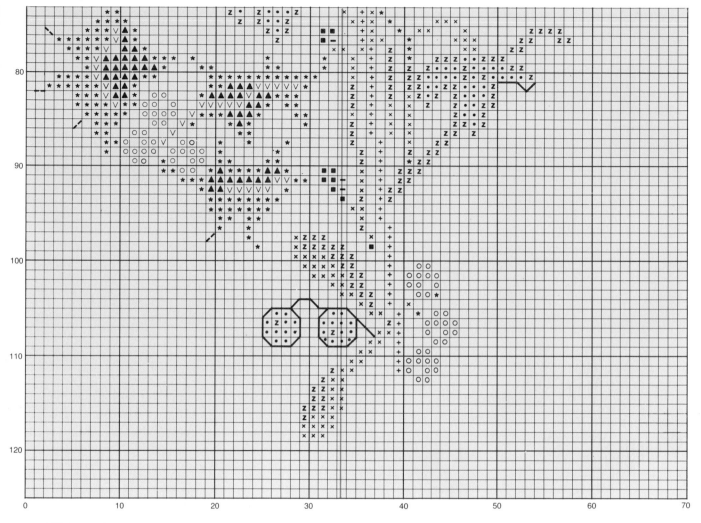

## Winter

- ■ Yellow
- – Rust
- / Brown
- ★ Dark green
- ● Dark red
- ○ Bright red
- □ Pink
- **e** Black

- ▼ Yellow sand
- z Light green
- • White
- × Green
- V Dull lt green
- ▲ Dull dk green
- + Mink brown

- △ Chocolate brown
- Dried flower head outlines in brown
- Dried flowers in rust
- Yew tree needles in shades of green
- progressively lighter towards tip
- Mistletoe berry outlines in light
- green

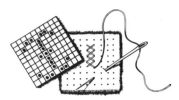

# BREAKFAST TRAYCLOTH

The fine count of the fabric and the small stitches
worked on it make this a design for the experienced needlewoman.
They also demonstrate that the smaller the stitch the lesser
the angularity of the design. The resulting soft outlines and delicate
shading produce a most realistic picture.

# CONSTRUCTION

The stitches are worked over one count of the fabric using one strand of cotton.

Work the border first, following the border charts below and opposite, which give the design repeat and four corner patterns. Start in the top left hand corner. Position the starting stitch, indicated on the chart below, 10 threads in from the top and 10 threads in from the side of the pre-edged line of stitches, if using a ready-made traycloth or 25 mm (1 in) in from the top and side edges, if using a piece of linen.

Work the border all around the four sides, adjusting the length to fit your tray.

Next work the motif. Starting at the top left hand border, count 81 threads down from the inside of the top border and 16 threads across from the inside of the left-hand border. Where the two lines meet is the position of the first stitch as marked on the chart on page 90. You may wish to run a line of tacking stitches in both directions to get the positioning right. Work the stems and pot outlines in running or back stitch.

When the stitching is completed, gently press the design on the reverse over a padded surface. If making your own traycloth, trim the fabric leaving a 1.5 cm (⅝ in) fabric border round the design, then bind the edges with bias binding.

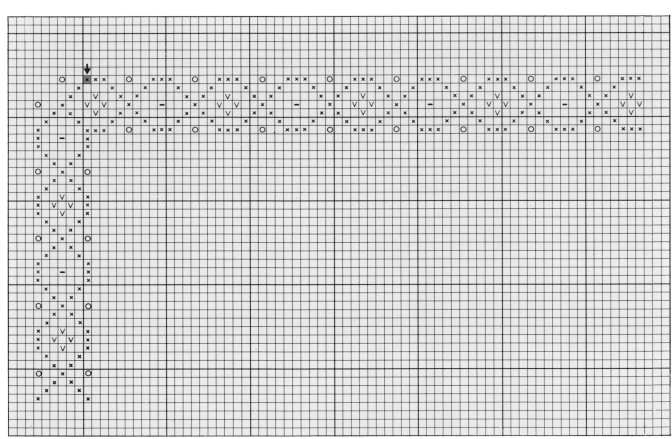

*Border chart showing start point and top left hand corner*

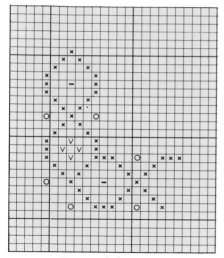

*Bottom left corner*

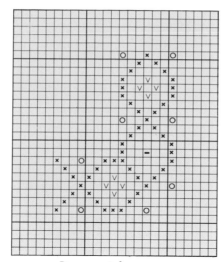

*Bottom right corner*

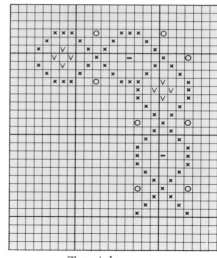

*Top right corner*

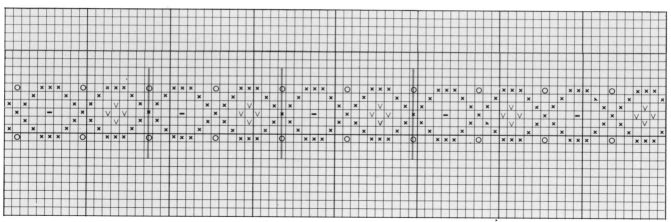

*Straight section showing border repeat*

## KEY

∧ Pale yellow
■ Pink
z Brown
▲ Light brown
▼ Peach
∨ Dark pink
× Blue
/ Light blue
+ Medium green
○ Light green

□ Light med. green
● Dark green
− Bright yellow
★ Very dk pink

Flower stalks in medium green
Pot cover outline in light blue
Jam pot outline in dark pink

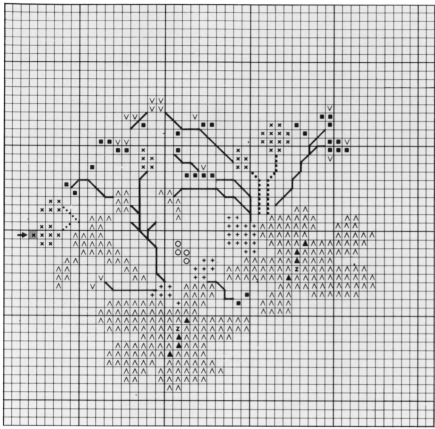

*Left: Traycloth motif. Above: Napkin motif*

at the point where these two lines meet. If you wish, you can repeat this motif in each corner of the napkin by turning the chart through 90° for each new motif. Finish the napkin in the same way as the traycloth.

## NAPKIN RING

### REQUIREMENTS

1 piece of cream even-weave fabric, as for the traycloth, 11 × 11 cm (4¼ × 4¼ in)
*or* 1 piece of Sal-EM for napkin ring, 26 count
1 napkin ring (page 93)
Stranded cottons and needle as for the traycloth

## MAKING UP

Make up your own motif by adapting the napkin motif. For example, take one of the yellow flowers and surround it with the little pink flowers. Design an overall shape to suit the napkin ring and place the design centrally on the fabric.

To complete, simply trim the fabric to fit and slip the piece into the napkin ring.

## EGG COSY

The motifs can of course be used in a wide variety of ways on linen for the breakfast tray or table. Try out the egg cup design on an egg cosy, for example.

## NAPKIN

### REQUIREMENTS

1 square piece of cream even-weave fabric, as for the traycloth, to your own dimensions
*or* 1 Sal-EM napkin (page 93)
Contrasting or toning bias binding (optional)
Stranded cottons and needle as for the traycloth

## MAKING UP

The stitches are worked over one count of the fabric using one strand of cotton.

Work the border in the same position on the napkin, as is described for the traycloth.

To position the motif from the chart above, count down 34 threads from inside the top border and 19 threads from inside the left-hand border. Position the first stitch of the flower

### FINISHING OFF

Fasten off each thread by darning the loose end into worked stitches on the reverse of the work.

When the whole design has been worked, snip off any loose ends of thread and either wash gently (see below) or press on the wrong side over a padded surface.

### PRESENTATION

Careful mounting will present your work in its best light.

Cards, gift tags, tree decorations: refer to the assembly instructions given with the Christmas project (page 24).

Pots and jars: back your design with a lightweight iron—on interfacing before cutting out and mounting. The interfacing will give the work body and prevent it from distorting and fraying as you mount it. To assemble the work, follow the manufacturer's instructions. It is a good idea to try out the instructions on a scrap of even-weave first.

Picture framing: it is well worth having this done professionally. Whether or not you have glass in your frame is a matter of personal choice. The glass protects the work and preserves it for future generations but also detracts from the subtle colours and textures of the needlework. A special spray can be used to give some protection to work mounted without glass.

Suggest to the framer that the work is backed with a piece of wadding.

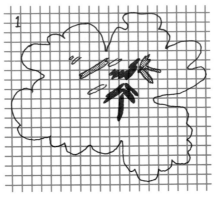

*The motif traced onto graph paper*

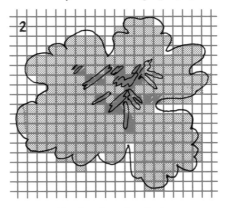

*Reshaping the design*

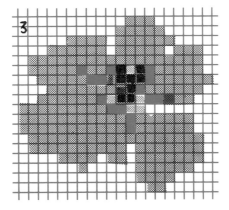

*Blocking in the different colours*

This provides a good base for the work to be stretched over and gives a softer line to the edges. Wadding has been used in this way for all the framed pieces in this book.

### Creating your own designs

You do not need to be a superb artist in order to make a successful design, since motifs traced from photographs, magazines or fabrics can be easily converted into chart form.

Having traced the chosen design, transfer this in pencil onto graph paper (diagram 1). Next, block round the outlines of the design following the squares of the graph paper (diagram 2). Lastly, fill in the shape, using pencil shading or coloured pencils for the different blocks of colour (diagram 3).

*N.B. Treat these colours only as a rough guide to the much wider range of shades which are available in cottons and silks.*

### CARE AND CONSERVATION

Do keep your work in a bag in between stitching sessions. Also store all threads and fabrics covered.

If the design has become a little grubby while you are working on it, gently wash it by hand in a soap-based detergent in warm water, unless you have been using pure silk threads, in which case the work must be dry-cleaned professionally. The stranded cottons recommended for the projects are colour-fast.

# GLOSSARY

**Aida** A type of *even-weave* fabric.

**Aida band** A type of *even-weave* fabric woven as a narrow band.

**Bias binding** A strip cut diagonally across the warp and weft threads of a piece of fabric.

**Binca** *Even-weave* fabric similar to *Aida* but with a coarser weave.

**Coton à broder/Brilliant embroidery cotton** A highly-twisted, fine cotton embroidery thread.

**Count** The number of holes per inch on an even-weave fabric.

**Even-weave fabric** Fabric woven with warp and weft threads of identical thickness providing the same number of threads over a given area.

**Oversewing/Overcasting** An embroidery stitch used to bind an edge.

**Perlé cotton/Pearl cotton** A twisted embroidery thread with a lustrous sheen.

**Stranded cotton/Embroidery floss** A loosely-twisted, six strand embroidery thread which can be separated for fine work.

**Tack, tacking/Baste, basting** A large, temporary running stitch.

**Wadding/Batting** Padding fabric made from cotton or synthetic fibres.

## ACKNOWLEDGEMENTS

With thanks to the following companies for their help with the photography:

Coats Leisure Crafts Group Ltd, 39 Durham Street, Glagow G41 1BS, U.K. (embroidery threads and fabrics)

Dunlicrafts Ltd, Pullman Road, Wigston, Leicester LE8 2DY, U.K. (embroidery threads and fabrics)

Fast Frame International Centre, Netherton Park, Stannington, Morpeth, Northumberland NE61 6EF, U.K. (mounting the embroidery)

Framecraft Miniatures Ltd, 148–150 High Street, Aston, Birmingham B6 4US, U.K. (products for embroidery)

## SUPPLIERS

Card blanks; Dressing table set; Lace-trimmed bookmarks; Mirror mounts; Napkin ring; Pots; Sal-EM fabrics; Tray mounts; Tree decorations.

Framecraft Miniatures Ltd, 148–150 High Street, Aston, Birmingham B6 4US, U.K.

Ireland Needlecraft Pty Ltd, 16 Mavron Street, Ashwood, Victoria 3147, Australia.

Anne Brinkley Designs Inc, 21 Ransom Road, Newton Centre, Mass. 02159, U.S.A.

Kits (i.e. fabric, needle, embroidery threads, excluding charts) for any of the projects in this book; card blanks; needlewoman starter pack.

'Stitchkits', 8 Danescourt Road, Tettenhall, Wolverhampton WV6 9BG, U.K.

# INDEX

PRINTED IN BELGIUM BY
proost
INTERNATIONAL BOOK PRODUCTION